MISSOURI ALMANAC 2018-19

Amanda E Doyle

Reedy Press
PO Box 5131
St. Louis, MO 63139
www.reedypress.com

Visit missourialmanacbook.com

Library of Congress Control Number: 2017934706

ISBN: 9781681061191

Design by Richard Roden

Printed in the United States

17 18 19 20 21   5 4 3 2 1

TABLE OF CONTENTS

FARMS, FOOD, BASEBALL, BIG CITIES, ROLLING COUNTRY, INNOVATION, AND INVENTION—IT'S ALL HERE IN MISSOURI!

Missouri's state flag was adopted on March 22, 1913. The twenty-four stars indicate that Missouri was the twenty-fourth state.

SEAL: adopted in 1822

OFFICIAL STATE SYMBOLS

POPULATION: 6,083,672 (ranked eighteenth)

BIRD: native bluebird

FOSSIL: crinoid
(*Delocrinus missouriensis*)

INSECT: honeybee

ANIMAL: Missouri mule

FLORAL EMBLEM: white hawthorn blossom

MINERAL: galena

MUSICAL INSTRUMENT: fiddle

ROCK: mozarkite

TREE: flowering dogwood (*Comus florida* L.)

TREE NUT: eastern black walnut

HORSE: Missouri Fox Trotter

AQUATIC ANIMAL: paddlefish

FISH: channel catfish

SONG: Missouri Waltz

DAY: third Wednesday in October

GRAPE: Norton/Cynthiana (*Vitis aestivalis*)

AMPHIBIAN: American bullfrog
(*Rana catesbeiana*)

REPTILE: three-toed box turtle
(*Terrapene carolina triunguis*)

GAME BIRD: bobwhite quail (*Colinus virginianus*)

INVERTEBRATE: crayfish (also known as crawfish
and crawdad)

DESSERT: ice cream cone

EXERCISE: jumping jack

Warsaw, Missouri, holds the state record for the lowest temperature: -40 degrees on February 13, 1905.

WAIT A MINUTE!

Warsaw also holds the record for the highest temperature: 118 degrees on July 14, 1954.

THE FIRST OLYMPIC GAMES HELD IN THE U.S. WERE IN ST. LOUIS DURING THE 1904 WORLD'S FAIR. IN THE MARATHON, NEARLY HALF OF THE RUNNERS GOT HEATSTROKE, AND THE PRESUMED WINNER CHEATED BY HITCHING A RIDE FROM MILE NINE TO MILE NINETEEN!

DURING ABRAHAM LINCOLN'S CAMPAIGN FOR THE PRESIDENCY, A STAUNCH DEMOCRAT NAMED VALENTINE TAPLEY FROM PIKE COUNTY, MISSOURI, SWORE THAT HE WOULD NEVER SHAVE AGAIN IF LINCOLN WAS ELECTED. TAPLEY KEPT HIS WORD AND DIDN'T SHAVE FROM NOVEMBER 1860 UNTIL HE DIED IN 1910. HIS BEARD GREW TO TWELVE FEET SIX INCHES LONG.

Nixa, Missouri, barber Finis Gold started Sucker Day in 1957.

Every year, Nixa residents take the day off school or work, and thousands of visitors come to partake in a heaping helping of the bottom-dwelling sucker fish.

ART AND ARCHITECTURE

CHAPTER 1

THE ST. LOUIS CATHEDRAL BASILICA IS NOT ONLY ONE OF ST. LOUIS'S MOST BEAUTIFUL BUILDINGS, BUT IT IS ALSO HOME TO AN ARTISTIC TREASURE. THE CHURCH HOUSES ONE OF THE WORLD'S LARGEST COLLECTIONS OF MOSAICS.

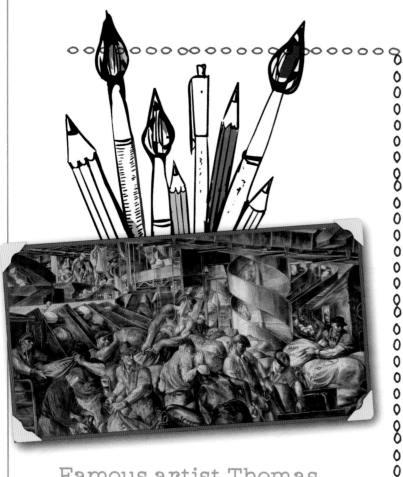

A NEW BUILDING MEETS AN OLD BUILDING AT THE NELSON-ATKINS MUSEUM OF ART IN KANSAS CITY.

The Nelson-Atkins Museum is what architects call a Beaux Arts–style building, and it has been around since 1933. But in 2007 an addition known as the Bloch Building gave the art museum a modern touch and filled it with natural light. The modern and African art collections are found in the Bloch Building.

Famous artist Thomas Hart Benton taught at the Kansas City Art Institute.

Thomas Hart Benton is one of Missouri's most famous artists. He is best known for his murals that show working people. His mural at the state capitol in the House Lounge depicts the state's highlights, such as agriculture and river commerce. It also illustrates Missouri's darker times, which included slavery and gangsters. His home in Kansas City is open to the public.

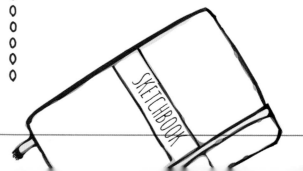

A NEW BUILDING WRAPS AROUND AN OLD BUILDING ON THE CAMPUS AT TRUMAN STATE UNIVERSITY.

This building is part of Truman State University. The original building was constructed in 1925, but twenty-five years ago a more modern building was constructed around it. New sunlit spaces for studying and reading are some of the features. Bridges and walkways allow visitors to go from the old building to the new one.

Concrete is the main feature of a science building in Springfield.

Temple Hall at Missouri State University in Springfield is a concrete building used for science classrooms and laboratories. What makes it unique is that the concrete was cast in place during the construction. The architects who designed the hall also designed the Kansas City airport; Kauffman Stadium, where the Royals play; and Arrowhead Stadium, where the Chiefs play.

THE GATEWAY ARCH
WEIGHS 43,226 TONS!

It's a symbol that's known around the world. The 630-foot-tall Gateway Arch was built as a reminder of how the United States expanded westward after the Louisiana Purchase. Eero Saarinen designed and created a monument with a lasting impression. Visitors can learn about the Arch's construction and the expansion. They can also tour the Arch grounds and the visitor center underneath, as well as take an elevator to the top for a view of the Mississippi River and beyond.

The courthouse in this small town in northeast Missouri is an example of Greek Revival architecture. It has four columns that are called Doric columns. The style was popular during this time and often included a porch and entry-way with columns.

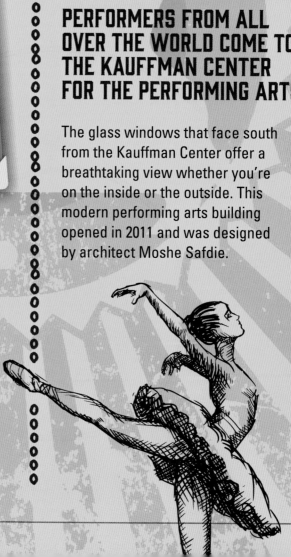

THE COLUMNS ON THE UNIVERSITY OF MISSOURI CAMPUS WERE SAVED FROM FIRE.

One of the most prominent landmarks in the state is the six columns in front of Jesse Hall on the University of Missouri campus. They are what remain from a fire that destroyed Academic Hall in 1892. Gideon F. Rothwell, the president of the board of curators at the time, insisted they keep the columns on campus. "Let the columns stand. Let them stand for a thousand years," he said.

PERFORMERS FROM ALL OVER THE WORLD COME TO THE KAUFFMAN CENTER FOR THE PERFORMING ARTS.

The glass windows that face south from the Kauffman Center offer a breathtaking view whether you're on the inside or the outside. This modern performing arts building opened in 2011 and was designed by architect Moshe Safdie.

KANSAS CITY AND ST. LOUIS PUBLIC LIBRARIES (MAIN, CENTRAL LOCATIONS)

People in Kansas City and St. Louis are called to the city's central library locations for more than books. Both libraries offer a lesson in beautiful architecture as well. A recent renovation of the St. Louis library included restoration of the chandeliers and installation of new wiring and lights to make it more modern. The Kansas City library *(pictured above)* includes a mix of styles from its special collections to its halls and film vault.

The historic Sappington House is in central Missouri.

The Sappington House near Arrow Rock is on the National Register of Historic Places. It's built in the Greek Revival style and features a central entrance doorway surrounded by wood. Parts of it have been restored over the years, but it still retains its architectural significance.

LAUMEIER SCULPTURE PARK IS FREE AND OPEN TO THE PUBLIC YEAR-ROUND.

It's a park and art all in one. Visitors can wander the park while seeing the latest ways that artists are experimenting in using modern art with the natural landscape. Pick up a guide and go explore the large structures and exhibitions on display.

Paint Louis invites graffiti artists to leave their mark on 1.9 miles of wall along the Mississippi riverfront.

Whether you call it graffiti or street art, if you look around St. Louis you'll see a lot of it. One of the city's prominent displays is the flood wall. For several years graffiti artists from across the country have come to St. Louis to paint the wall south of the Gateway Arch.

Kansas City has nearly fifty fountains that are operated by parks or the city.

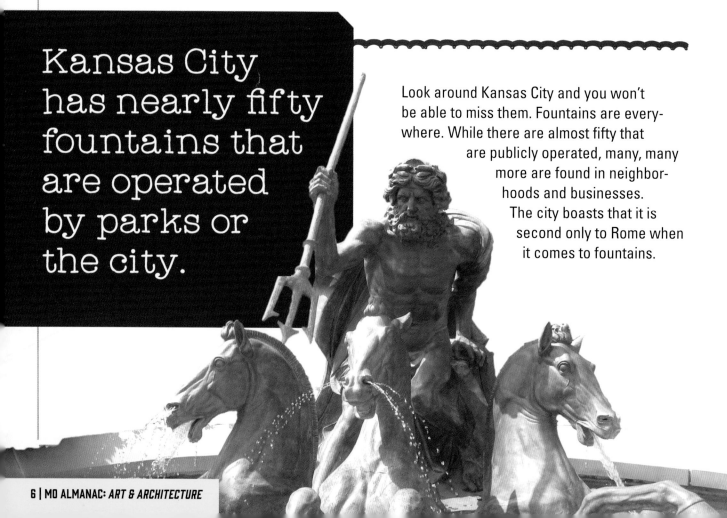

Look around Kansas City and you won't be able to miss them. Fountains are everywhere. While there are almost fifty that are publicly operated, many, many more are found in neighborhoods and businesses. The city boasts that it is second only to Rome when it comes to fountains.

POWELL SYMPHONY HALL IN ST. LOUIS SEATS 2,683.

The wonders of classical music meet the beauty of architecture when we talk about the state's two symphony orchestras. In St. Louis, Powell Symphony Hall *(shown at right)* is home to the St. Louis Symphony Orchestra. The Kansas City Symphony finds a place at the Kauffman Center for the Performing Arts, which is known as one of the world's top performing arts venues.

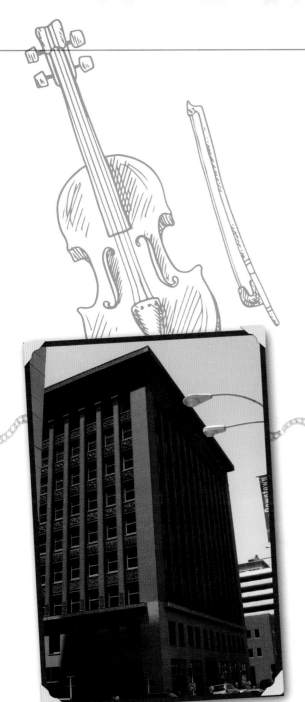

THE WAINWRIGHT BUILDING WAS ONE OF THE FIRST MODERN HIGH-RISE BUILDINGS.

This building in downtown St. Louis is historic because it's considered to be one of the first skyscrapers. Louis Sullivan designed it in 1892. Modern office buildings were later built in the style of the Wainwright Building. The building became a state office complex in the early 1980s.

THERE ARE FIVE FRANK LLOYD WRIGHT HOMES IN MISSOURI.

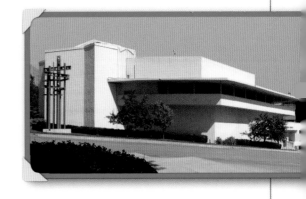

Missouri is home to five homes of famous architect Frank Lloyd Wright. The Kraus House in Kirkwood, constructed mostly of glass, wood, and brick, was built for an artist and his wife. The Theodore A. Pappas House in St. Louis includes concrete blocks held together with rebar. Other places where Wright left his mark are the Bott House, the Community Christian Church *(shown here)*, and the Clarence Sondern House in Kansas City.

ANIMALS

CHAPTER 2

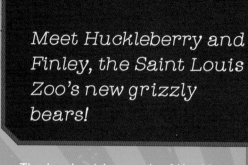

Meet *Huckleberry and Finley, the Saint Louis Zoo's new grizzly bears!*

The brother/sister pair of Huckleberry and Finley came from Montana to live in the new Grizzly Ridge habitat in St. Louis. Notice the "blonde" grizzled coat on this bear, which is how grizzly bears got their name.

Twister the Horse

IF IT WERE NOT FOR THE ACCIDENT, TWIST OF FATE WOULD NEVER HAVE BEEN BORN.

A tractor trailer carrying horses bound for slaughter crashed on Interstate 44 in 2006. One of the victims of this wreck was Mama, a pregnant thoroughbred mare. Mama was rescued and taken to Longmeadow Rescue Ranch where she gave birth to a healthy colt aptly named Twist of Fate and known as Twister.

LiLY, a WeimaRaNeR FROM JOPLiN, MiSSOURi, iS a SeaRCH aND ReSCUe DOG.

Lily the Hero Rescue Dog

Lily is trained to pick up on human scent. After a category EF5 tornado hit her hometown in 2011, Lily went out into the streets with her owner Tara and helped people who had been hurt by the storm.

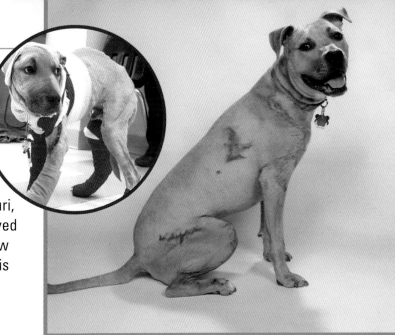

IN 2012, A PIT BULL PUPPY WAS TIED TO A TRUCK AND DRAGGED FOR A MILE DOWN THE HIGHWAY.

Rescued by the Humane Society of Missouri, the pup was named Trooper after he survived and recovered from his ordeal. Trooper now has a forever home in St. Louis, and with his owner, Greg, acts as an advocate against animal abuse.

HER CAT, LAVERN, WAS ALIVE AND BURIED IN THE RUBBLE!

Lavern the Cat

When Terrla Cruse returned to her home in Joplin, sixteen days after it was hit by the 2011 tornado, she saw that it was completely destroyed. But then she heard a faint meowing. Terrla rescued the thirteen-year-old miracle cat, who eventually made a complete recovery.

JiM WAS FAMOUS FOR RESPONDING TO ANY QUESTION OR COMMAND.

Jim the Wonder Dog

Jim the Wonder Dog of Marshall, Missouri could identify trees, license plates, or a single person in a crowd. He could even predict the future! Scientists never solved the mystery of his amazing abilities.

The HSMO was founded in 1870, so it's actually more than 140 years old!

The Humane Society of Missouri provides a safe place for animals in need by giving them shelter, veterinary care, and a chance to get adopted by a family.

THE APA IS A GREAT PLACE TO ADOPT A NEW FRIEND.

In 1922, Ella Megginson saw a man beating his horse in Webster Groves, Missouri. She decided to do something about it. Ella started the Animal Protective Association of Missouri in order to prevent cruelty and act as advocates for animals.

DID YOU KNOW THAT AT THE HUMANE SOCIETY OF MISSOURI KIDS CAN READ TO DOGS?

The Shelter Buddies Reading Program helps pets become more adoptable by teaching them to be calm around people. Plus, kids get to practice their reading and make a furry friend too!

More than two thousand patients are treated each year, including turtles, opossums, raccoons, various birds, and more.

Wildlife Rescue Center in Ballwin, Missouri, works to rehabilitate injured, sick, and orphaned animals from the wild.

THE STAFF OF GATEWAY PET GUARDIANS CARES FOR STRAY ANIMALS FOUND IN EAST ST. LOUIS.

Animals are fed, rescued, given veterinary care, and placed in foster homes on the road to adoption in forever homes.

I LOVE DOGS

DID YOU KNOW THAT YOU CAN SEE BALD EAGLES RIGHT HERE IN MISSOURI?

About two thousand of these incredible birds pass through in the winter. The many big rivers, lakes, and wetlands in Missouri make our state an attractive home for our national bird.

MISSOURI'S LARGEST POPULATION OF BOBCATS LIVES IN THE OZARK REGION.

Bobcats are the most common wildcat found in North America, and you can recognize them by the big tufts of fur on their ears. Bobcats are predators that hunt small mammals and birds but they will also scavenge for meat when it's available.

TROUT FISHING IS A VERY POPULAR SPORT IN MISSOURI.

Introduced to Missouri in 1882, rainbow trout have to live in water that is colder than 70 degrees, so in Missouri they can be found in spring-fed streams. They are called rainbow trout because of the long, pink stripe on their sides.

Black bears are native to Missouri, and their populations are making a comeback.

Black bears hibernate in the wintertime and feed throughout the summer. These bears are omnivorous, so they will eat almost anything! It is important to never feed a bear. Bears must be kept wild for their safety and yours.

Coyotes can be found in both urban and rural areas.

The coyote is a very adaptable member of the canid family. (That means it's related to wolves and dogs.) Coyotes are nocturnal predators, but they can occasionally be seen during daytime hours as well.

They are carnivores, eating small mammals, but will scavenge for whatever is available, particularly in cities.

DID YOU KNOW THAT NINE-BANDED ARMADILLOS CAN BE FOUND IN MISSOURI?

They've been moving farther north and have been observed living in our state since 1980. The name armadillo means "little armored one." The name suits these small mammals, as they are covered in a shell made out of true bone that looks—and works—just like a suit of armor, protecting them from harm.

OPOSSUMS ARE THE ONLY MARSUPIAL FOUND IN NORTH AMERICA.

That means they carry their babies in pouches, just like kangaroos! They are scavengers who will eat almost anything with their fifty teeth. They have semi-prehensile tails, meaning they can use them to wrap around things and help them climb, but they cannot sleep while hanging from their tails for long periods of time.

Raccoons are famous for the black fur around their eyes that makes them look a little like tiny bandits.

They have very nimble paws, allowing them to catch crawfish or even open a garbage can. Like opossums, they will eat almost anything, and they are very good climbers.

WHITE-TAILED DEER ARE VERY COMMON IN BOTH RURAL AND SUBURBAN PARTS OF MISSOURI.

They are typically very shy and will wave their white tails back and forth when startled. Their antlers are used against other male white-tailed deer in competition for females during the breeding season. They are usually crepuscular, meaning they're most active at dawn and dusk.

BOX TURTLES GET THEIR NAME FROM THEIR UNIQUE ABILITY TO CLOSE UP INSIDE THEIR SHELL LIKE A BOX.

The plastron (or bottom shell) is hinged so it can close up against the carapace (upper shell). These turtles, found in woodlands throughout the state, can actually live to be fifty to eighty years old!

North American river otters are a conservation success story in Missouri.

In 1980, there were only about fifty or so otters in our state. Otters were reintroduced to Missouri by bringing in healthy animals from Louisiana. Today there are more than 15,000 otters! They are very intelligent, playful animals and are also skilled hunters known to catch a lot of fish.

TODAY, THERE ARE
MORE THAN 15,000 OTTERS!

THE SAINT LOUIS ZOO IS A FREE ZOO LOCATED IN FOREST PARK IN ST. LOUIS.

Here you can see and learn about more than 17,000 animals, including lions, tigers, elephants, rare hellbenders and horned guans, and, of course, Kali the playful polar bear. The Saint Louis Zoo works to conserve animals in the wild by supporting conservation projects through its thirteen WildCare Institute centers across the globe.

YOU CAN MEET THE ANIMALS UP CLOSE AND PERSONAL AT DICKERSON PARK BY SIGNING UP FOR ONE OF THEIR UNIQUE ANIMAL ENCOUNTERS.

The Dickerson Park Zoo can be found in Springfield, Missouri. It is set on one hundred acres and even includes a veterinary hospital that is dedicated to rehabilitating native wildlife in need.

The Endangered Wolf Center in Eureka, Missouri, was founded by TV personality Marlin Perkins and his wife, Carol Perkins, more than forty years ago.

The EWC is dedicated to wild canid conservation, including Mexican wolves, red wolves, African painted dogs, and fox species. The EWC has even released animals born there into the wild!

HERE YOU CAN VISIT 1,300 ANIMALS IN KANSAS CITY'S SWOPE PARK.

The Kansas City Zoo was founded in 1909 and is divided into five themed areas—Africa, Australia, Tiger Trail, KidZone, and the Valley.

GRANT'S FARM IS ACTUALLY A STATE HISTORIC SITE, AS THE PROPERTY WAS ONCE OWNED BY THE EIGHTEENTH PRESIDENT OF THE UNITED STATES, ULYSSES S. GRANT.

Grant's Farm is home to elephants, buffalo, camels, kangaroos, goats, parrots, donkeys, peacocks, and—most famously—the Budweiser Clydesdales. Visitors can see a bird show or elephant training demonstration, as well as feed goats in the busy goat yard.

Lone Elk Park is a St. Louis County park where elk and bison were released in 1948.

Today visitors can drive through the park and observe these large, hooved animals as they roam through the woodland. You can also see deer, waterfowl, wild turkey, and bison.

THE WORLD BIRD SANCTUARY IN EUREKA, MISSOURI, COMBINES RESCUE, RESEARCH, REHABILITATION, AND EDUCATION FOR A VARIETY OF BIRD SPECIES.

The bird sanctuary was founded by Walter Crawford more than forty years ago. Here you can see eagles, hawks, and other birds of prey, as well as parrots, pelicans, and even a bat named Batty!

PADDLEFISH ARE NATIVE TO THE MISSISSIPPI RIVER.

The largest paddlefish on record was twenty-three feet long! Today, paddlefish populations are declining due to overfishing, pollution, and human development.

The mule was officially designated as the Missouri state animal in 1995.

A mule is the offspring of a female horse and a male donkey. Mules are strong and hearty animals, known for pulling wagons. Missouri has always been the primary mule producer in the U.S.

The eastern bluebird is the state bird of Missouri.

OFFICIAL
MISSOURI STATE BIRD!

You can recognize a male bluebird by its bright blue feathers and pinkish/red chest. The females have a greyish tint to their feathers. Bluebird eggs are a pale shade of blue.

KALI WAS ORPHANED IN THE WILDS OF ALASKA IN 2013.

Kali was taken to the Buffalo Zoo to live with another polar bear cub named Luna. Luna and Kali grew up together until he was about two and a half years old. He then moved to the Saint Louis Zoo where he can be found splashing and diving in one of his saltwater pools!

THESE LARGE DRAFT HORSES ARE CAPABLE OF PULLING A ONE-TON LOAD AT FIVE MILES PER HOUR!

The famous Budweiser Clydesdales made their first public appearance in 1933 and have been a symbol of St. Louis majesty ever since.

BABY ORANGUTANS HAVE A LONG CHILDHOOD AND WILL STAY WITH THEIR MOTHER FOR UP TO SEVEN YEARS.

Ginger was born in December 2014. Her mom, Merah, is one of the oldest-known orangutan mothers in captivity. She's the mother of five, grandmother of two, and great-grandmother of one!

RAJA WAS THE FIRST ELEPHANT TO EVER BE BORN AT THE SAINT LOUIS ZOO.

The River's Edge habitat at the zoo was actually built so the zoo could house a bull elephant, following Raja's birth. Now Raja is the father of four daughters—Maliha, Jade, Kenzi, and Priya.

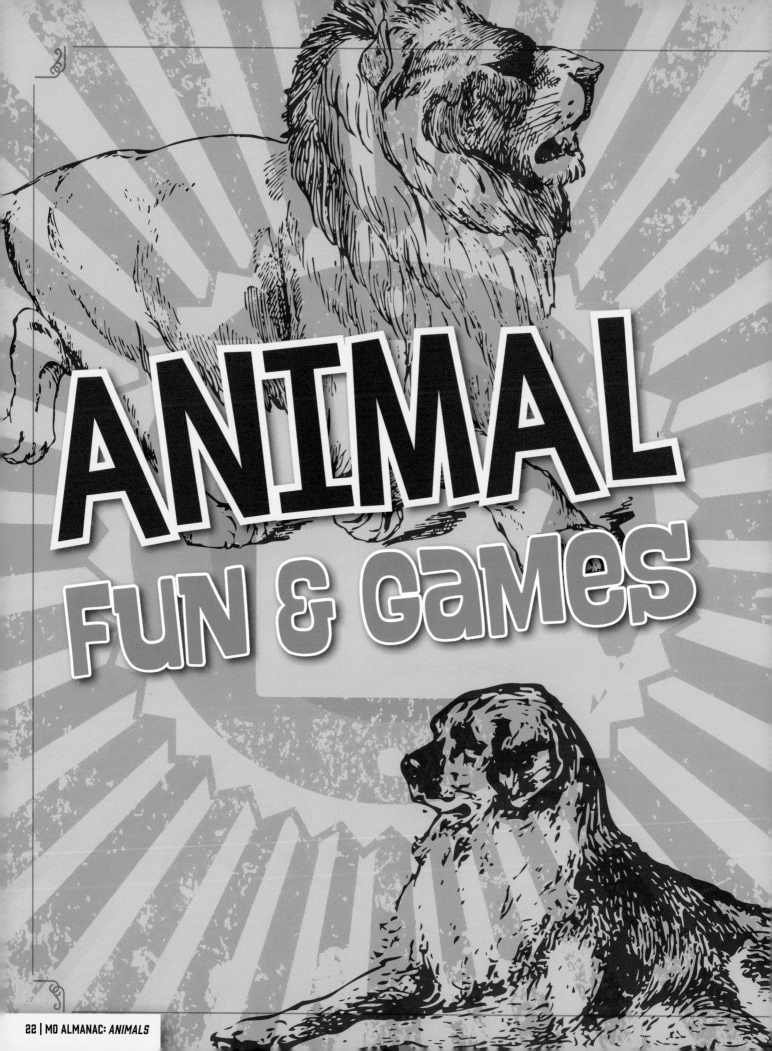

ANIMAL
FUN & GAMES

Across

1. IF YOU WANT TO SEE ME, YOU BETTER GET UP VERY EARLY IN THE MORNING.

2. DON'T BELIEVE THE CARTOONS. I CAN'T SLEEP HANGING BY MY TAIL.

3. IN SPITE OF MY NAME, I'M NOT REALLY SQUARE.

Down

1. I DON'T NEED A TOUPEE. THERE ARE FEATHERS UP THERE.

2. NO NEED TO BE FORMAL AND CALL THIS CAT "ROBERT."

3. I'M OMNIVOROUS, SO DON'T WAKE ME FROM MY WINTER NAP OR YOU MIGHT BE DINNER.

4. WOLVES AND DOGS ARE MY COUSINS.

5. I'M COVERED IN A SHELL, BUT I'M NOT A TURTLE.

6. I LIKE A MIDNIGHT SNACK FROM YOUR TRASH CAN.

7. I'M NOT JUST CUTE. I'M VERY SMART AND GREAT AT FISHING.

ANSWERS IN BACK OF BOOK

SHOW ME THE DIFFERENCE

UNSCRAMBLE NAMES OF THESE MISSOURI ANIMALS.

1. rocanoc _____

2. teoyco _____

3. xob utelrt _____

4. btcboa _____

5. soopusm _____

6. issiromu leum _____

7. clkab abre _____

8. rwaobin tuort _____

9. sphilfddea _____

10. nien-adbned imarodall _____

11. nertaes bdeuirbl _____

12. eihtw-litdae dere _____

13. ierrv orett _____

ANSWERS IN BACK OF BOOK

THE FARM

CHAPTER 3

Stuckmeyers Farm Market and Greenhouse
STUCKMEYERS IS THE PLACE TO PICK A PUMPKIN.

With hayrides, pony rides, farm animals, and lots and lots of pumpkins, it's a great family-friendly farm for a fall afternoon.

Green Dirt Farm

GREEN DIRT FARM BELIEVES THAT HAPPY EWES MAKE THE BEST MILK, so they always follow Animal Welfare Approved's strict standards—including giving the sheep lots of pasture to graze in and large herds to socialize with. Green Dirt Farm makes delicious cheese and hosts farm tours and events.

Thies Farm

EVERY FALL, THIES FILLS UP WITH PUMPKINS OF EVERY SHAPE AND SIZE, as well as haystack slides and mazes and some farm animals to meet too. It's the perfect place to kick off the Halloween season.

Weston Red Barn Farm

Classes and families visit the Weston Red Barn Farm to pick apples, peaches, and pumpkins and learn about farm life.

The farm's owner, Steve Frey, decided to buy the farm so that he could recreate the memories he made playing on his own uncle's farm when he was a child. The farm is located in Weston, Missouri.

SHATTO MILK COMPANY IS A DAIRY FARM JUST NORTH OF KANSAS CITY.

It's family owned and operated, and the milk is always fresh and bottled in glass. You can even tour the farm or attend one of their many fun-filled events.

Purina Farms

You can meet a lot of fun animals at Purina Farms.

There are pigs and rabbits to pet and a cow to milk, as well as a cat house and dog kennel. Don't forget to check out the dog agility course, where dogs jump, zig, zag, and dodge obstacles. If you're lucky, you might even catch a dog show while visiting Purina Farms.

SUSON FARM HELPS KIDS WHO LIVE IN URBAN AREAS GET A SMALL TASTE OF WHAT LIFE IS LIKE ON A FARM.

Suson Farm is located inside Suson Park in south St. Louis County. Here, you can visit real farm animals like horses, cows, sheep, and pigs.

WARM SPRINGS RANCH IN BOONVILLE, MISSOURI, IS ONE OF THE HOMES OF THE FAMOUS BUDWEISER CLYDESDALES.

This is a breeding ranch, so lots of baby horses, called foals, are born here. Clydesdales weigh around 125 pounds at birth, but they grow to be between 1,600 and 2,200 pounds! You can meet the Clydesdales by taking a tour of Warm Springs.

THE GROW EXHIBIT AT THE ST. LOUIS SCIENCE CENTER IS ALL ABOUT FOOD.

We all know that food is delicious and essential to our daily needs, but this exhibit goes a little deeper, exploring where food comes from and the journey it takes to get from the farm to the table.

EARTH DANCE FARM IN FERGUSON, MISSOURI, IS HOME TO A "FARM SCHOOL" OF SORTS.

This apprenticeship program teaches students about organic agriculture, or farming without using pesticides and other chemicals. Apprentices are out in the fields growing food, learning from farmers, and even helping to sell the fruits of their labor at the market.

FARM SCHOOL!

The Doris I. Schnuck Children's Garden at the Missouri Botanical Garden

This Children's Garden brings plants and nature to life with a "Missouri in the Nineteenth Century" theme. You can play in cave-, wetland-, and steamboat-themed areas, as well as climb into a treehouse or visit a Midwestern prairie village.

SOYBEANS ARE THE MOST IMPORTANT CROP IN MISSOURI.

Soybeans can be used to make vegetable oil or feed for cattle, or they can be eaten—as in tofu, soy sauce, or edamame. Soybean sales in Missouri have often been more than one billion dollars a year!

MOST OF THE CORN GROWN IN MISSOURI IS USED TO MAKE FEED FOR FARM ANIMALS.

Missouri is a corn exporter. This means that our state ends up sending corn to other places rather than using it here.

Wheat can be used to make breads, cereals, and pasta, among other things.

Wheat is a cereal grain crop. Missouri grows two types of wheat—the western third of the state grows hard red winter wheat, and the eastern two thirds of the state grows soft red winter wheat.

GROWING HAY IN MISSOURI ALSO HELPS TO FEED FARM ANIMALS.

Hay is simply grass that has been cut and dried for animal feed. Cattle, horses, goats, and sheep can eat hay in winter when there's not enough grass for them to eat in the pasture.

COTTON

Missouri grows a type of cotton called upland cotton, which is the most common type of cotton grown in the U.S.

ONE BALE OF COTTON CAN WEIGH UP TO **FIVE HUNDRED POUNDS!**

GRAIN SORGHUM

Farmers also grow grain sorghum in Missouri. Grain sorghum looks similar to corn, and like corn it can be used to make food for farm animals.

Schweizer Orchards
Located in St. Joseph, Missouri

THIS FARM HAS BEEN IN THE SCHWEIZER FAMILY FOR FOUR GENERATIONS,

and they are known for their delicious apples. At Schweizer Orchards, you can pick apples, buy fresh produce at their market, or even take a farm tour and explore the orchard and straw maze.

THIS NORTHEAST MISSOURI FARM BOASTS 2,200 BLUEBERRY PLANTS RIPE FOR PICKING!

The Lost Branch Blueberry Farm provides recipes for making your own blueberry jams, cakes, scones, pancakes, and more.

The Berry Patch

The Berry Patch is a pick-your-own blueberry farm in Cleveland, Missouri, just south of Kansas City. Aside from picking fresh, delicious blueberries, you can enjoy an obstacle course and playground, and you can even ride around the farm on the Berry Train!

RIDE THE BERRY TRAIN!

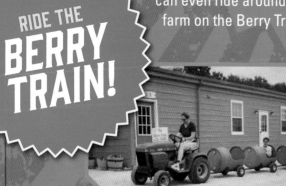

HERITAGE VALLEY TREE FARM

Pick your own pecans and apples at Heritage Valley Tree Farm in Washington, Missouri, and then return in the winter to cut down your own Christmas tree! This farm has been family owned for more than one hundred years.

G's Orchard

THIS ORCHARD IS PROUD TO SELL LOCALLY GROWN, FRESH PRODUCE AND BEEF.

G's Orchard is in Verona, Missouri. Here you can pick blueberries, peaches, apples, cantaloupes, and even a few vegetables like tomatoes and peppers.

John and Linda's fruit and berry farm

At John and Linda's farm in Bates City, Missouri, you can pick and eat strawberries, peaches, apples, blackberries, and pears.

MULE BARN BERRIES

At Mule Barn Berries, you can pick raspberries, strawberries, and blackberries, and you can also taste some of their delicious jams and jellies.

There are many organic farms in Missouri.

Organic farmers choose not to use pesticides, fertilizers, or genetically modified organisms during their farming process. You can find an organic farm near you by going to the website eatwild.com.

Monsanto is a large agricultural company based in St. Louis.

On the opposite end of the spectrum from organic farming, Monsanto was one of the first companies to create genetically modified crops (GMCs). GMCs are plants whose DNA has been changed so that they are larger and more nutritious or resistant to certain pests—among other possibilities.

LOTS OF MISSOURIANS ARE TRYING TO EAT LOCAL FOODS.

Local foods are items that are grown or raised in our state, so they are both fresh and better for the environment since they don't have to be shipped as far to get to the grocery store. You might find a local farm near you in this section of this almanac.

FARM organic MEAT eggs & milk

THE U.S. HAS A LONG HISTORY OF FAMILY FARMING.

But in today's world, with advanced technology, many farmers can grow more crops on large corporate farms rather than on a small family farm without the same access to state-of-the-art advances. Many families depend on their farms, but more crops mean more food for those who need it. So what do you think? Are small or large farms better for Missouri?

THE OUTDOORS

CHAPTER 4

MISSOURI HAS BEEN THE LOCATION OF SIX OF THE TWENTY-FIVE DEADLIEST TORNADOES IN U.S. HISTORY.

A tornado is simply a rotating column of air that forms a funnel. You can see the funnel because it's full of water, dust, and debris.

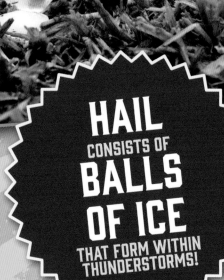

HAIL CONSISTS OF BALLS OF ICE THAT FORM WITHIN THUNDERSTORMS!

Hail is much more common than tornadoes but can also be dangerous. Most hail is tiny, but a strong thunderstorm called a supercell can create hail stones the size of softballs!

DID YOU KNOW WE ACTUALLY HAVE FREQUENT SMALL EARTHQUAKES IN MISSOURI?

Missouri sits on the New Madrid Seismic Zone—a part of the U.S. where two parts of the Earth's crust come together like a crack in an eggshell. A series of earthquakes in New Madrid, Missouri, in the early 1800s were some of the most intense quakes to ever occur on this continent.

SNOWSTORMS

Average annual snowfall in Missouri can vary tremendously. For example, Caruthersville's average in the south is as little as 2.3 inches, while Rolla in central Missouri gets 18.9 inches. But the Missouri record for biggest snowfall has to go to Cape Girardeau, which was covered in 24 inches of snow on February 25, 1979.

Thunderstorms are very common in Missouri, especially in the spring and summer months.

What's the difference between a thunderstorm watch and a thunderstorm warning? Watches are typically guesses of where and when a thunderstorm might occur, while warnings mean that the storm is about to arrive in a certain area.

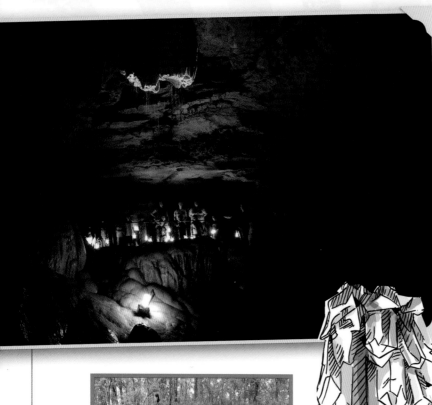

DID YOU KNOW THAT MISSOURI IS KNOWN AS THE CAVE STATE?

That's because Missouri is home to more than six thousand caves, second only to Tennessee!

MORE THAN 6,000 CAVES!

Spelunking means to explore caves.

Many people make it a hobby. Some caves in Missouri are large and meant for tourists, while other smaller caves are meant to be explored by expert spelunkers.

YOU SHOULD MOVE SLOWLY AND CAREFULLY WHEN EXPLORING A CAVE.

If you're going into a smaller cave, it's important to be safe! Wear pants, long sleeves, and a hard hat with a mounted light. You should bring along at least two more lights per person since caves can be very dark. Wear boots with good traction, and bring along some gloves.

The outlaw Jesse James was even known to use this cave as a hideout!

Meramec Caverns is a 4.6-mile cave system located in the Ozarks. You can take a guided tour through Meramec Caverns. Keep your eye out for several famous features, like the Wine Table, the Stage Curtain, the Hollywood Room, the Ballroom, and the Mirror Room.

IT'S THE OLDEST OPERATING SHOW CAVE IN THE STATE.

Mark Twain Cave is located in Mark Twain's childhood home of Hannibal, Missouri, and it inspired certain passages in Mark Twain's most famous book, *The Adventures of Tom Sawyer*.

ONONDOGA CAVE

Onondaga Cave is located just outside Leasburg, Missouri. You can take a tour of some of Onondaga Cave's spectacular geologic formations, such as the Queen's Canopy, the Twins, and the Lily Pad Room.

Rivers are a very important part of Missouri history.

When Europeans first came to Missouri, they settled along the riverbanks where they could farm, ship goods by boat, and trap animals for fur. Today, rivers are still a very important part of the state—for people, wildlife, and our environment.

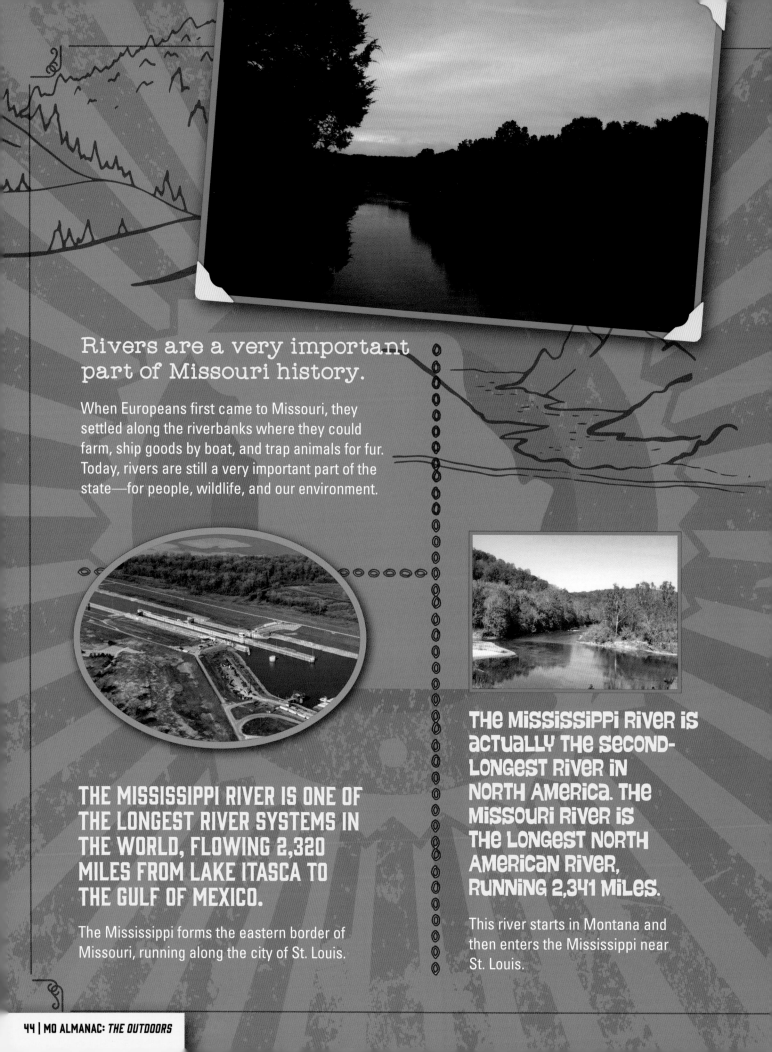

THE MISSISSIPPI RIVER IS ONE OF THE LONGEST RIVER SYSTEMS IN THE WORLD, FLOWING 2,320 MILES FROM LAKE ITASCA TO THE GULF OF MEXICO.

The Mississippi forms the eastern border of Missouri, running along the city of St. Louis.

THE MISSISSIPPI RIVER IS ACTUALLY THE SECOND-LONGEST RIVER IN NORTH AMERICA. THE MISSOURI RIVER IS THE LONGEST NORTH AMERICAN RIVER, RUNNING 2,341 MILES.

This river starts in Montana and then enters the Mississippi near St. Louis.

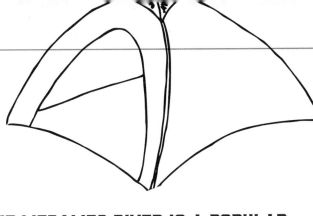

THE MERAMEC RIVER IS A POPULAR CANOEING, FLOATING, AND CAMPING DESTINATION FOR MANY MISSOURIANS.

The Meramec River runs from Salem until it empties into the Mississippi River near St. Louis.

THE ST. FRANCIS RIVER

This St. Francis River starts at Elephant Rocks State Park, where you can explore the giant boulders and watch the river as it begins its 426-mile-long journey.

THE CURRENT RIVER

The Current River runs through the southeastern area of the Ozarks. It's a popular river for camping, floating, horseback riding, and fishing.

CAMPING IS A GREAT WAY TO EXPLORE THE OUTDOORS.

Families and friends can cook food (including s'mores!) over a campfire, sleep under the stars, and enjoy the quiet and fresh air. Missouri offers lots of great camping opportunities.

MISSOURI IS HOME TO FORTY-ONE STATE PARKS THAT OFFER 3,600 CAMPSITES— SO THERE ARE PLENTY OF PLACES TO CHOOSE FROM WHEN CAMPING IN MISSOURI!

RULES FOR CAMPING

Missouri promotes the idea of "Leave No Trace" when camping. This means campers must follow certain rules:
- Plan ahead and prepare for your camping trip
- Camp on durable surfaces
- Dispose of waste properly
- Leave what you find
- Minimize campfire impacts
- Respect wildlife
- Be considerate of other visitors

BETWEEN ITS LAKES AND RIVERS, MISSOURI OFFERS LOTS OF FISHING OPPORTUNITIES!

You can catch everything from little bluegill, to fresh trout, to a big ol' largemouth bass. Be sure to read about local fishing laws before you head out though. Most state parks will have catch limits in place.

WHEN YOU'RE PLANNING OUTDOOR CAMPING, HUNTING, AND FISHING ACTIVITIES, A GREAT RESOURCE IS THE MISSOURI DEPARTMENT OF CONSERVATION.

The MDC's website will let you know when certain seasons have started and how to get permits, and the site also highlights the natural beauty of Missouri's wildlife and environment.

MISSOURIANS LOVE BOATING & WATER SPORTS!

Boaters here can tube, waterski, jet ski, fish, or simply relax and catch some rays.

MOST HUNTERS TYPICALLY HUNT DEER, TURKEYS, WATERFOWL, OR GAME BIRDS.

Hunting is a popular sport in Missouri. Just like with fishing, it's important to check seasons and regulations before planning a hunt.

KATY TRAIL PARK

The Katy Trail includes a "Rails to Trails" trail, which means that an old railroad was converted into a biking/hiking trail for everyone to enjoy. The Katy Trail is 240 miles long and runs along the Missouri River through most of the park.

Mastodon State Park

Mastodon State Park is near Imperial, Missouri. This park's claim to fame is the Kimmswick Bone Bed. Excavations of the bone bed have led to some very important archaeological discoveries, including the remains of mastodons and giant ground sloths found alongside stone spear points from the Clovis culture. This discovery offered some of the first evidence of humans living alongside giant, prehistoric beasts.

BABLER STATE PARK

Just outside St. Louis, Babler Park offers miles of hiking/biking/ horseback riding trails and plenty of places to enjoy a picnic.

HAWN STATE PARK

One of the prettiest of Missouri's state parks, Hawn is located just outside Ste. Genevieve, Missouri. Hiking trails wind around the park, lined by beautiful streams and pine and oak forests.

Ha Ha Tonka State Park is a favorite in Missouri because of its beautiful views and unique castle.

That's right—Ha Ha Tonka State Park is home to the remains of a castle built by a Kansas City businessman at the turn of the twentieth century. This park is in the Lake of the Ozarks.

THIS PARK TOTALLY ROCKS!

The highlight of any trip to Elephant Rocks is, of course, scrambling across the giant boulders, lined up end to end like a parade of elephants. The boulders were formed from 1.5-billion-year-old granite!

A SHUT-IN IS ACTUALLY AN OZARK TERM FOR A RIVER WITH A DEEP, NARROW CHANNEL.

These rivers have strong rapids and can't be canoed, making boaters "shut in." Johnson's Shut-Ins has plenty of giant boulders to climb on while enjoying the beauty of the Black River or a perfect picnic spot.

Castlewood is a favorite park of residents of St. Louis and the surrounding area.

In the early 1900s, Castlewood was a popular place to go for a party. That era is gone, but many visitors still enjoy Castlewood's winding trails and beautiful bluffs overlooking the Meramec River.

QUEENY PARK

Queeny Park in St. Louis County is home to wooded trails, a fun playground, and even a recreation complex. Queeny also hosts several equestrian events each year. This park was once the estate of Edgar Queeny. Edgar was a former president of Monsanto and the son of Monsanto's founder, John Queeny.

TURTLE PARK

Turtle Park is home to seven large concrete turtles and one snake. You can see the turtles on the right side whenever you are heading east on Highway 40 near Forest Park in St. Louis.

CREVE COEUR PARK

Creve Coeur Park is not only the largest St. Louis County park, but it also contains Creve Coeur Lake—the largest natural lake in Missouri.

CAVE SPRING PARK

Cave Spring Park near Kansas City has a lot of fun options. You can take a cave tour in Current River Cavern, take a ride on one of the two zip-line courses, or even dig for real minerals and fossils in the quarry!

TOWER GROVE PARK SERVES 2.5 MILLION CHILDREN AND ADULTS EACH YEAR, THE MAJORITY FROM URBAN NEIGHBORHOODS IN ST. LOUIS.

Tower Grove Park was founded by merchant Henry Shaw in 1868, as a gift to the city of St. Louis. Shaw did have a few requirements though. He said that it "shall be used as a park forever" and that an "annual appropriation" be made by the city "for its maintenance." To this day, Tower Grove Park is a beautiful urban green space, full of trees, flowers, bridges, and even a music stand that hosts yearly concerts for everyone to enjoy.

FOREST PARK

Forest Park is one of the most beautiful city parks in the U.S. It covers a whopping 1,293 acres and St. Louis gems like the Saint Louis Zoo, the History Museum, the Art Museum, and the Science Center—not to mention plenty of trees, lakes, and green space.

FOREST PARK BIGGER THAN NY'S CENTRAL PARK!

FOREST PARK WAS ALSO HOME TO THE WORLD'S FAIR AND OLYMPICS IN 1904.

Loose Park was the site of the Battle of Westport during the Civil War.

Loose Park is a large park in Kansas City. The park is full of picnic areas, a rose garden, a water park, and even some Civil War history!

WATERFALL PARK

Located just across a lake from the Bass Pro Shop in Independence, Missouri, Waterfall Park features a playground, a rock climbing wall, and plenty of beautiful trails to explore.

PENGUIN PARK

Penguin Park in Kansas City includes the usual park amenities, like a playground and picnic tables, but it also includes a giant fiberglass penguin and a few other large animal friends. The penguin and a giraffe were installed in the mid-1960s, but plenty of people still enjoy visiting the giant penguin and his park today.

CAPE GIRARDEAU CONSERVATION NATURE CENTER'S GOAL IS TO GET PEOPLE OUTSIDE.

The nature center encourages everyone to participate in outdoor activities, like hunting, fishing, hiking, gardening, and bird-watching.

CLARENCE CANNON NATIONAL WILDLIFE REFUGE IS FOR THE BIRDS—LITERALLY!

Located in the floodplain of the Mississippi River in Pike County, lots of bird species can be found here, including waterfowl, wading birds, songbirds, and even shorebirds.

YOU CAN HIKE IN THE WOODS, WORK IN THE SCIENCE LAB, OR EVEN JOIN THE STAFF FOR ONE OF MANY CONSERVATION-RELATED ACTIVITIES.

Located near Kansas City, Lakeside Nature Center is a great place to learn about native Missouri wildlife. Not only does Lakeside work to rescue and rehab native animals, but it also offers great classes for students and scouts.

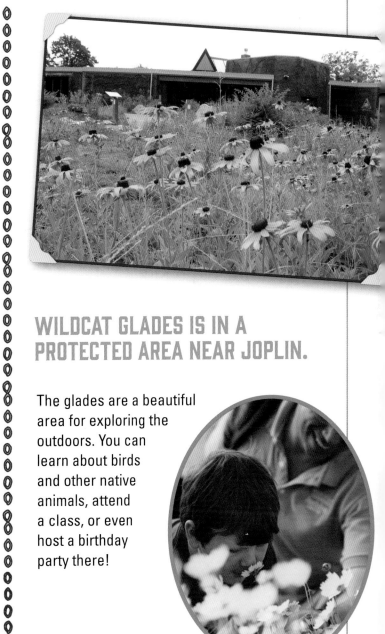

MISSOURI ACTUALLY SHARES THE TWO RIVERS NATIONAL WILDLIFE REFUGE WITH ILLINOIS.

The refuge was founded in 1958 to protect the habitat of migratory birds. The refuge is located on a floodplain and wetland. It's a great place to spot lots of different bird species, including bald eagles in the winter.

WILDCAT GLADES IS IN A PROTECTED AREA NEAR JOPLIN.

The glades are a beautiful area for exploring the outdoors. You can learn about birds and other native animals, attend a class, or even host a birthday party there!

FUN & GAMES

OUTDOORS MAZE

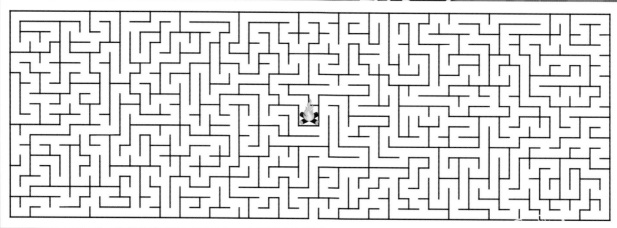

SHOW ME THE DIFFERENCE

WEIRD LAWS

FOLLOWING ARE SOME WEIRD LAWS THAT HAVE BEEN PASSED IN MISSOURI. DON'T WORRY, MOST OF THESE ARE NO LONGER LAWS.

COLUMBIA, MISSOURI
• Clotheslines are banned, but clothes can be draped over a fence.

ST. LOUIS
• A milkman may not run while on duty.

KANSAS CITY
• Installation of bathtubs with four legs resembling animal paws is prohibited.

PURDY
• Dancing is strictly prohibited.

MOBERLY
• It's illegal to race a stagecoach down Rollins Street.

MISSOURI (STATEWIDE)
• You need to have a permit to shave while driving.

• Single men between the ages of twenty-one and fifty must pay an annual tax of one dollar.

• It is illegal to smoke a pipe through your ear.

• It is illegal to eat clam chowder on Sunday between 11:50 a.m. and 12:48 p.m.

• Worrying about squirrels is not tolerated.

• One may not honk another person's horn.

ANSWERS IN BACK OF BOOK

FAMOUS MISSOURIANS

CHAPTER 5

Maya Angelou (1928-2014)

AMONG THE JOBS IN HER LIFE, MAYA ANGELOU WAS A CALYPSO DANCER, A FRY COOK, AN OPERA SINGER, AND A TELEVISION SHOW WRITER.

The celebrated writer penned poetry, memoirs, essays, and journalism during her long career. She was also well known as a civil rights activist, demanding fair and equal treatment for black people. Angelou spent much of her early childhood in tiny Stamps, Arkansas, but returned to her hometown of St. Louis when she was eight. The country girl was almost overwhelmed by the hustle and bustle of the big city. In her memoir *I Know Why the Caged Bird Sings*, she wrote: "I had decided that St. Louis was a foreign country. I would never get used to the scurrying sounds of flushing toilets, or the packaged foods, or doorbells or the noise of cars and trains and buses that crashed through the walls or slipped under the doors."

Thomas Hart Benton (1889–1975)

BEFORE HE PAINTED HIS PANORAMIC MURALS, THOMAS HART BENTON FIRST BUILT AN ENTIRE CLAY MODEL OF THE SCENE HE WANTED TO CAPTURE.

Thomas Hart Benton led an artistic movement known as regionalism, in which he painted pictures of everyday people doing ordinary daily activities, from unhitching a plow horse to dancing in the living room. Born in Neosho, as an adult he also lived and worked in Joplin and Kansas City. He pursued drawing and painting from an early age, working as a newspaper artist, attending art school, and moving to Europe to learn his craft. Some of his most popular works are murals on the walls of public buildings that you can still visit today (see more on p. 2).

Daniel Boone (1734–1820)

DANIEL BOONE

According to Boone family lore, Daniel had a luxurious cherry-wood coffin made for himself and would periodically inspect and lie down in it (while he was alive!) to make sure it still fit.

One of the most famous of all American frontiersmen, Daniel Boone was born in Pennsylvania and also spent time in North Carolina, Florida, and Virginia. Most famously, though, Boone was the champion explorer and settler of Kentucky. He was part of a team of about thirty men who hacked their way through dense wilderness to create a two-hundred-mile path known as the Wilderness Road through the Appalachian Mountains to Kentucky. He helped found forts and defended them against Native Americans who were upset that the new settlers had taken over their hunting grounds. He was the subject of a bestselling (and somewhat embellished) book about the history of Kentucky, which helped him become a global celebrity and folk hero while he was still alive. Boone came to present-day Missouri, which was then a Spanish territory called Upper Louisiana, in the 1790s, to live near Defiance in a home built by his son Nathan. He lived his remaining years there and died in what's now known as the Daniel Boone Home in 1820. Visit the site and the surrounding historical village to get a glimpse of frontier life.

Yogi Berra (1925–2015)

"Yogi" was born Lorenzo Pietro Berra but got his nickname from a teammate who said he looked like a Hindu yogi when he sat waiting to bat, arms and legs crossed.

Favorite son of St. Louis's Italian neighborhood known as "the Hill," Yogi Berra made his mark in baseball's major leagues as a stellar catcher who also hit like a champ. The street where he grew up, Elizabeth Avenue, was also home to baseball legend Joe Garagiola and sports broadcaster Jack Buck. Berra is in the sport's hall of fame in part because he played on more championship teams than any other player. He also had a career after his playing days, as a coach and a team manager. His family members accepted the Presidential Medal of Freedom from President Barack Obama on Berra's behalf in 2015.

Susan Blow (1843–1916)

Susan Blow spent fifteen months in Brazil, starting in 1869, working as her father's secretary when he was appointed U.S. ambassador to the South American country.

When most of us think about kindergarten, we think of how much fun it was to play and learn all day with lots of colorful blocks, toys, and other tools. Before Susan Blow, though, kindergarten as we know it didn't exist in the United States. As the highly intelligent and well-educated daughter of a wealthy local family, Blow had the chance as a young woman to travel the world. In Germany, she saw how schools for very young children used simple objects like balls and blocks to let them explore concepts in math, science, and language. She wanted to bring that experience to her hometown of St. Louis, so she convinced the head of public schools there to let her open an experimental public kindergarten in 1873. It was the first in the nation, and the popular model quickly spread through the city and across the country. A model of the first kindergarten classroom set up by Blow is open for tours at the Carondelet Historical Society.

T. S. Eliot (1888–1965)

Although he eventually became a British citizen and lived most of his life outside the U.S. T. S. Eliot said of St. Louis. "I feel that there is something in having passed one's childhood beside the big river. which is incommunicable to those people who have not. I consider myself fortunate to have been born here. rather than in Boston. or New York. or London."

Thomas Stearns (T. S.) Eliot, known to his friends as "Tom," was a modernist poet, playwright, and literary critic who grew up in St. Louis. During his lifetime, he had an imposing reputation as a literary giant; he won the Nobel Prize for Literature in 1948. His long poem *The Waste Land* was published in 1922, and many people think it was the most important poem of the twentieth century. He often wrote about the loneliness and disconnection that young people felt from the world (in the aftermath of World War I); one famous line from *The Waste Land* reads, "I will show you fear in a handful of dust." Eliot himself struggled with despair and depression at times, but he also had happy episodes in his life. He even wrote a lighthearted book of poems, *Old Possum's Book of Practical Cats*, which became the basis for the wildly popular Broadway musical *Cats*.

George Washington Carver (1861?–1943)

GEORGE WASHINGTON CARVER WAS THE FIRST AFRICAN AMERICAN TO HAVE A NATIONAL MONUMENT DEDICATED IN HIS HONOR: A SITE NEAR DIAMOND, MISSOURI, WHERE HE LIVED AS AN ENSLAVED CHILD, WAS FOUNDED IN 1943.

No one would have guessed at the future achievements of George Washington Carver when he was born into slavery on a western Missouri plantation in the mid-1800s. His year of birth is not even clearly established, because enslaved men, women, and children were considered property, not people, at that time. His father and mother were owned by a white couple, Moses and Susan Carver. His father and mother both died when he was an infant, and he was essentially raised and even educated at home by his owners, even after the end of the Civil War freed former slaves. Even his name came from them: he was originally known as "Carver's George," a reference to his status as an owned person, but it became George Carver when he finally went to a nearby school. He excelled at science and arts, which formed the basis for his lifelong obsession with botany (the study of plants) and the natural world. He was nicknamed "the plant doctor," and he made history with his college and advanced degrees from a school that had never had a black student before. He researched and taught many agricultural topics, even developing a "mobile classroom" in a vehicle to take his lessons to farmers in the field. He also became widely known as "the peanut man," due to his more than one hundred inventions and innovations based on the simple peanut. From paints to a kind of gasoline, Carver saw unlimited potential in the crop. He lectured and worked in labs and the field for his entire life, and he remains one of the best-known American innovators.

100+ PEANUT INVENTIONS

Walt Disney
(1901–1966)

Walt's most famous character, Mickey Mouse, almost didn't become a household name, at least not with that name! When twenty-seven-year-old Walt Disney first sketched a mouse character, he gave it the name Mortimer Mouse. His wife talked him into the breezier "Mickey."

Walt Disney's name resonates more than fifty years after the man himself died because of the continuing worldwide success of the brand he created. Disney, who lived in Marceline and Kansas City when he was a boy, was an artist, animator, and entrepreneur. He produced scores of films, including *Cinderella, Peter Pan, Lady and the Tramp, Fantasia, One Hundred and One Dalmatians,* and *Mary Poppins.* He holds the record for the most Academy Awards earned by an individual (22). Disney loved drawing from the time he was quite young. Throughout his career, he helped introduce innovations like full-color Technicolor and full-length animated features to the film industry. He also, of course, branched out into the world of amusement parks, opening Disneyland and Disneyworld (in California and Florida), where the central area, "Main Street, USA," was designed to replicate the main street of Marceline, Missouri.

MICKEY'S ORIGINAL NAME WAS "MORTIMER MOUSE"!

Kate Chopin (1850–1904)

KATE CHOPIN'S ACCLAIMED BOOK *THE AWAKENING* IS THE MOST FREQUENTLY ASSIGNED AMERICAN NOVEL TO ENGLISH CLASSES IN THE UNITED STATES . . . EVEN THOUGH IT WAS WRITTEN IN 1899!

Her name at birth in St. Louis was Catherine O'Flaherty, but the part-Irish/part-French writer known to the world was Kate Chopin. She grew up bilingual in French and English and later completely immersed herself in the Creole culture throughout New Orleans and elsewhere in Louisiana, after she married a Louisiana man and moved there. The Chopins had six children (five boys and a girl) within eight years, and when her husband died in 1882, Kate was left alone to raise them all. She brought her family back to St. Louis, where they lived in the Central West End neighborhood and Kate began to write fiction. Her books and stories often focused on women and their complex emotions, even for those living fairly ordinary lives. Her two novels, *At Fault* and *The Awakening*, were not thought much of when they were published, but fifty years after her death, they found new audiences and her work enjoyed an incredible revival. Chopin also published collections of stories about Creole life and people who lived in the Louisiana bayou. She even wrote stories for children's magazines. Chopin died in 1904 after returning from an extremely hot day at the St. Louis World's Fair. She is buried in the city's Calvary Cemetery.

Brad Pitt (born 1963)

BRAD PITT DROPPED OUT OF COLLEGE AT THE UNIVERSITY OF MISSOURI–COLUMBIA TWO WEEKS BEFORE HE WOULD HAVE GRADUATED FROM JOURNALISM SCHOOL.

Film actor/director/producer Brad Pitt grew up in Springfield and as a kid enjoyed roaming the natural areas around his home. In high school, he participated in debate, sports, and the occasional school musical. Instead of finishing his college degree, he headed to California and began acting in small parts for soap opera television shows. He gained major attention for a minor role in the movie *Thelma & Louise* and went on to star in a wide variety of films, including *A River Runs through It*, *Fight Club*, and *Troy*. Pitt is also hugely interested in architecture and has spent some of his non-acting/directing time and resources setting up environmentally friendly affordable housing competitions. In addition to his career, he has a long list of charitable causes close to his heart.

FROM "LET AMERICA BE AMERICA AGAIN," JULY 1936

"O, LET AMERICA BE AMERICA AGAIN—THE LAND THAT NEVER HAS BEEN YET—AND YET MUST BE—THE LAND WHERE EVERY MAN IS FREE. THE LAND THAT'S MINE—THE POOR MAN'S, INDIAN'S, NEGRO'S, ME—WHO MADE AMERICA, WHOSE SWEAT AND BLOOD, WHOSE FAITH AND PAIN, WHOSE HAND AT THE FOUNDRY, WHOSE PLOW IN THE RAIN, MUST BRING BACK OUR MIGHTY DREAM AGAIN."

Langston Hughes (1902–1967)

Langston Hughes wrote lyrical, emotionally rich poems about the lives and everyday experiences of African American people, and his poems show great influence from jazz music, which he loved. He also wrote novels and plays. He was a leading figure in the artistic movement based in New York called "the Harlem Renaissance," which was a period of black pride and celebration (through literature, music, and other arts) in the 1920s and '30s. He was born in Joplin, but a family split sent him to several other Midwestern towns before high school. Just two years out of high school, in 1922, he published his first poem, "The Negro Speaks of Rivers," written just outside St. Louis as he observed the Mississippi River from a train. That poem, and others like "Let America Be America Again" and "My People," offered a glimpse into the proud, complicated history of the black experience in America and the world.

Walter Cronkite (1916–2009)

A NATIONAL POLL ONCE NAMED WALTER CRONKITE "THE MOST TRUSTED MAN IN AMERICA" . . . ABOVE EVEN THE PRESIDENT AND VICE PRESIDENT OF THE UNITED STATES.

Walter Cronkite knew from the time he was twelve years old that he wanted to be a journalist (foreign correspondent was his chosen niche, after he read about the career in a *Boy's Life* magazine article), and he never wavered from his goal. Born in St. Joseph, he worked for several small newspapers and radio stations before making a significant mark as a wire service reporter for a news organization called United Press. (Wire services are news-gathering agencies that report stories and then send them out for mass distribution by other newspapers, websites, and TV networks.) Cronkite became a household name, though, by being a television anchor in the early days of the *CBS Evening News*, from 1961 until he retired twenty years later. He was known for his calm and steady demeanor while delivering even the most significant news (including the assassination of President John F. Kennedy) and for his desire and willingness to go into the situations he was reporting on, including into active war zones.

Scott Joplin (1868?–1917)

SCOTT JOPLIN IS ONE OF JUST A HANDFUL OF PEOPLE TO RECEIVE A PULITZER PRIZE POSTHUMOUSLY (AFTER DEATH). HIS SPECIAL AWARD IN 1976 HONORED "HIS CONTRIBUTIONS TO AMERICAN MUSIC."

SCOTT JOPLIN DEVELOPED THE MUSICAL STYLE RAGTIME!

One of six children born to former slaves in Texas, Scott Joplin made his way north, performing music on the piano, violin, and cornet, as well as singing. He ended up making Sedalia his home base in 1893, for what he hoped would be a noteworthy career as a musical composer. He gained fame for his "rags," a new form of lively melody combined with offbeat rhythms (syncopation) that were a craze in the 1920s and '30s. Joplin moved to St. Louis to further his career and continued writing music and teaching, although he stopped performing as much. He wrote works including "The Maple Leaf Rag," "The Entertainer," and "Cascades," which was commissioned for the opening of the 1904 St. Louis World's Fair. He also wrote scores for operas, although he ran into many obstacles getting them produced onstage (including the racism common everywhere that made it hard for him to access money and venues to put on shows.) He left a vast legacy in ragtime, a uniquely American art form. Today, Sedalia hosts an annual Scott Joplin Ragtime Festival, and in St. Louis you can visit the Scott Joplin House State Historic Site.

C. BECHSTEIN.

Charles Lindbergh (1902–1974)

CHARLES LINDBERGH'S WIZARDRY AT MECHANICS AND ENGINEERING CAME IN HANDY OUTSIDE HIS AIRPLANE. INSPIRED BY HIS SISTER-IN-LAW'S BATTLE WITH HEART DISEASE, HE TEAMED UP WITH A FRENCH PHYSICIAN AND IN 1935 PERFECTED A GLASS PUMP SYSTEM THAT COULD HELP KEEP HUMAN ORGANS ALIVE OUTSIDE THE BODY. THEIR WORK GAVE A BOOST TO THE EVENTUAL DEVELOPMENT OF ARTIFICIAL BODY PARTS AND SAVED LIVES.

Lindbergh Flies Atlantic

32 USA
1998

"Lucky Lindy," as he was dubbed by the international media, made the first successful, nonstop solo flight across the Atlantic Ocean in May 1927. The feat had been tried by many, and his touchdown on a Paris airfield, in a plane called the *Spirit of St. Louis*, thrilled people all over the world. During his brief time living in St. Louis after he graduated from army air school, he had made connections with businessmen who had both money and aviation connections. They agreed to pay for his plane for the attempted transatlantic flight, and Lindbergh named it in gratitude to them. Prizes, awards, parades, and fame followed. Lindbergh lived a life of both triumph (he was a stunt pilot, a military veteran, a champion of scientific causes from rocketry to conservation) and tragedy (his infant son was kidnapped and murdered in a sensational crime case, and he was accused of being a Nazi because he did not want the U.S. to enter World War II.) A replica of the *Spirit of St. Louis* hangs in the Missouri History Museum Grand Hall.

Annie Turnbo Malone (1859–1967)

Annie Malone wanted success for more than just herself: she was also a crusader for the economic progress of other black people. She used her own money to buy jewelry and other rewards for her employees who sold her products, and she invested in property in St. Louis.

Annie Malone used her natural abilities in chemistry to found a groundbreaking hair products company in the early 1900s, and its success made her one of the nation's first African American millionaires. As a black woman entrepreneur, the usual channels of sales and distribution were not open to her, so Malone cleverly marketed her Poro hair products through a social network of assistants going door to door to demonstrate their power. Her sales grew steadily, and she reinvested proceeds to grow the business nationally. She opened Poro College in St. Louis in 1918 as a cosmetology and business hub, and by the mid-1950s there were branches in thirty-two other towns and cities. She was a generous benefactor of charities, including the St. Louis Colored Orphans Home, which was renamed the Annie Malone Children and Family Service Center in her honor.

Marlin Perkins (1905–1986)

MARLIN PERKINS WAS HIRED TO ACCOMPANY SIR EDMUND HILLARY'S 1960 EXPEDITION CLIMBING MOUNT EVEREST. HIS JOB WAS TO INVESTIGATE REPORTS AND EVIDENCE OF THE ABOMINABLE SNOWMAN! TURNS OUT, THE OVERSIZED FOOTPRINTS WERE JUST MELTED TOGETHER TRACKS OF SMALLER ANIMALS, LIKE FOXES.

Zoologist Marlin Perkins made his mark both locally and nationally. Born in Carthage, he spent most of his adult life in St. Louis, where he was the second full-time director of the Saint Louis Zoo and at the same time developed the wildly popular television show *Mutual of Omaha's Wild Kingdom*. On the show, he went over snowy mountain ranges and under the sea's surface, taking viewers for a close-up look at species and habitats many had never seen. A lifelong animal lover, he'd started collecting for his own "zoo" at the age of seven (mostly snakes, toads, and mice he found on the family farm) but was put in charge of the zoo's reptile collection and grew the number of specimens on display from six when he started to more than five hundred, just eleven years later. Perkins was a tireless voice for conservation and animal protection even after he retired from the Saint Louis Zoo.

Harry S. Truman (1884–1972)

HARRY TRUMAN HAD A MIDDLE INITIAL ("S") BUT NOT A MIDDLE NAME: HIS PARENTS CHOSE IT TO APPEASE BOTH HIS GRANDFATHERS, WHO HAD "S" NAMES.

Harry Truman served as the thirty-third president of the United States and is regarded by historians as one of the best presidents in our history. A lofty achievement for a young boy born in Lamar and raised in Harrisonville, Grandview, and Independence. He excelled at school but his poor eyesight kept him out of sports and even a chance to go to college at the United States Military Academy at West Point. Instead, he read widely and helped run his family's farm after the death of his father. Truman served in World War I, and after the war returned to Missouri to get married, raise a daughter, and try (and fail) at several business ventures. He first entered politics in 1922, when he became an elected judge in Jackson County. His career took him to the U.S. Senate, and then he became vice president under Franklin Roosevelt (who had just been reelected.) Quite unexpectedly, Roosevelt died just a few months later, moving Truman into the presidency. During his term in office, he oversaw the country's involvement in World War II, made a controversial decision to drop atomic bombs on Japan to try to end the war, created alliances to encourage cooperation among nations, and ended racial segregation in the military. He did not run for a second term as president but returned to Independence to write his memoirs and establish the Truman Presidential Library & Museum.

Laura Ingalls Wilder (1867–1957)

Although she was nearly thirty years old when she and her husband first came to Missouri, settling on a farm outside Mansfield, Laura Ingalls Wilder made the state her home for the rest of her long life.

She began writing here, and when she did, she captivated young readers with the tales of everyday life, along with adventure and hardship, growing up on the American frontier in the late 1800s. From devastating blizzards and desperate illness to unique sights like cattle drives and Indian reservation life, Wilder was able to draw on her own childhood with her frontier family to bring the experiences alive.

Little House in the Big Woods was the first in her multi-book Little House series . . . and she didn't publish it until she was sixty-five! She continued writing professionally her whole life, with the editing and marketing help of her daughter Rose. Her legacy and life are celebrated at the preserved home and a museum in Mansfield.

Dred (1799?-1858) and Harriet (1815?-1876) Scott

THE FIRST AND ONLY STATUE IN THE WORLD OF DRED AND HARRIET SCOTT IS IN DOWNTOWN ST. LOUIS AND CAME ABOUT THROUGH THE EFFORTS OF THEIR GREAT-GREAT-GRANDDAUGHTER LYNN JACKSON, WHO STILL LIVES IN THE AREA.

Enslaved married couple Dred and Harriet Scott were living in St. Louis when they filed their first lawsuits seeking freedom in 1846. Having been taken into free territory (where slavery was not legal) by several of the families that had owned them, they sued based on the accepted practice known as "once free, always free." This idea had been well established in the courts by previous successful lawsuits by former slaves. Their case was lost, retried, won, appealed, and finally lost again. Out of options at the state level, the Scotts took their quest to the United States Supreme Court. In 1857, they lost again, when the Supreme Court returned an infamous verdict in the case officially known as *Scott v. Sandford*. Among other things, it said:

• The original authors of the Constitution did not intend for blacks to be considered citizens.

• They had no rights that citizens would have.

Since the Scotts were not citizens, they were not allowed to use the nation's court system. This decision set off a firestorm of controversy that contributed, ultimately, to the Civil War.

After the Supreme Court decision, the Scotts' owner immediately sold them back to a former (sympathetic) owner, who freed them and their children right away. Dred lived less than a year, but he spent his final months as a free man. Harriet lived almost another twenty years. Both are buried in St. Louis cemeteries.

Mark Twain (1835–1910)

"Mark Twain" is a pseudonym that was used by the real man behind the name, Samuel Clemens. Although he became well known as Twain, it wasn't his only pen name. At other times in his writing career, he went by W. Epaminondas Adrastus Blab and Thomas Jefferson Snodgrass.

Born in the tiny town of Florida, Samuel Langhorne Clemens, aka Mark Twain, soon moved with his family to nearby Hannibal, and his boyhood growing up along the Mississippi River in this port city shaped much of the rest of his life. He played along its banks and met the people who came and went on the riverboats passing through. During his young adulthood, Twain worked in various jobs in the newspaper and publishing industries and then decided to train as a riverboat pilot. In 1861, when his brother was sent west by President Abraham Lincoln, Twain tagged along and tried to strike it rich as a silver miner. He had no success and returned to a job he knew: he became a newspaper reporter in Nevada. He traveled to San Francisco and began writing humorous stories that got published across the country and gained him a big audience. He took up public speeches to promote his work and make money for his travels. He went to Europe and wrote *Innocents Abroad*, his first best-selling book. After he married and settled in Connecticut, he had four children (three of whom died young). In Connecticut, he wrote the two books for which he is most remembered, *The Adventures of Tom Sawyer* and *The Adventures of Huckleberry Finn*, largely based on his boyhood in Hannibal. His keen observations about human behavior and sly ways of poking fun at social and political hot topics made him a wildly popular author and speaker. He and his family moved to Europe for a time but returned to the U.S. in 1900, where he lived until his death.

Tennessee Williams (1911–1983)

TENNESSEE WILLIAMS WON TWO PULITZER PRIZES AND THE PRESIDENTIAL MEDAL OF FREEDOM.

Playwright Tennessee Williams (born Thomas Lanier Williams) moved to St. Louis from Mississippi with his family as a young boy. His parents had very different personalities and temperaments and fought constantly, a dynamic of family dysfunction that came up frequently in Williams's work. He graduated from high school in University City and attended Mizzou's journalism school. His father made him leave college to return to work in the shoe factory he managed. Tennessee turned more seriously to writing and eventually graduated from the University of Iowa with an English degree. He began traveling. After years of trying, he had a successful play when *The Glass Menagerie* was performed in Chicago and then produced on Broadway in New York. Other important works followed, including *A Streetcar Named Desire*, *Cat on a Hot Tin Roof*, and *Sweet Bird of Youth*. Despite the acclaim, Williams struggled his whole life with unresolved family issues, drug and alcohol abuse, and mental illness. His legacy is acknowledged today in an annual theater festival in St. Louis. He is buried in the city's Calvary Cemetery, despite frequently speaking of his dislike of his time growing up in St. Louis.

Sam Walton (1918–1992)

As an entrepreneur with business in several states, Sam Walton decided that buying a small airplane and learning to pilot it would make it easier to check in on his stores.

Sam Walton, along with his brother James "Bud" Walton, pioneered modern discount shopping and founded the mega-retailers Wal-Mart and Sam's Club. Sam moved with his family to Springfield when he was five and later lived in Marshall, Shelbina, and Columbia, where he graduated from high school as the "Most Versatile Boy" in his class. All during his school years, he worked several jobs and participated in extracurricular activities. After graduating from Mizzou, Walton took a job with J. C. Penney as a retail manager trainee. World War II service interrupted that path, but after the war he again returned to the world of shopping, opening first a Ben Franklin franchise and then Walton's Five & Dime in Bentonville, Arkansas. His guiding principles, including always putting the customer first and buying in bulk to get steeply discounted products, were honed in these experiences. In 1962, the first true Wal-Mart store opened in Arkansas. From that single store, a worldwide empire grew to be worth many billions of dollars. It helped catapult the Walton family to the top of the list of America's wealthiest people, although Sam continued to live quite frugally.

FUN & GAMES

FAMOUS MISSOURIANS WORD SEARCH

```
W  H  H  H  Y  M  T  Q  Z  E  Y  A  S  F  M  R  T  Y  U  B
N  P  C  A  A  V  A  N  T  E  N  N  Y  W  B  E  H  H  J  H
I  T  O  S  V  R  K  R  N  I  I  O  P  V  N  K  L  E  E  Z
P  K  D  Z  U  K  R  S  K  K  W  S  L  N  W  R  S  B  Q  Q
O  K  V  X  H  B  I  Y  R  T  U  F  E  A  L  A  I  O  D  V
H  V  D  H  U  D  S  E  S  S  W  S  Z  A  M  P  F  S  K  R
C  Q  P  R  T  B  P  U  A  T  S  A  C  Q  H  E  H  M  O  V
E  B  A  L  M  N  Q  N  H  E  R  M  I  A  E  I  I  D  N  K
T  M  A  A  I  P  B  C  E  P  A  U  R  N  B  L  Y  N  T  Z
A  W  N  L  S  L  I  W  X  Y  L  X  M  D  D  R  S  S  N  D
K  J  R  L  O  N  I  K  A  F  G  O  P  A  A  A  K  A  U  A
V  A  D  W  C  L  C  A  G  E  M  R  D  M  N  H  Z  M  U  V
M  Y  P  Z  L  K  N  A  J  B  G  O  X  A  I  C  H  W  J  A
E  T  H  I  H  G  R  E  B  D  N  I  L  S  E  L  R  A  H  C
O  D  A  L  E  C  A  R  N  E  G  I  E  Y  L  H  I  L  Q  J
M  M  Q  L  D  R  E  D  S  C  O  T  T  L  B  Y  Y  T  A  E
S  N  O  N  I  L  P  O  J  T  T  O  C  S  O  C  F  O  A  W
R  U  O  Q  F  F  P  Z  D  Z  D  D  R  U  O  P  M  N  W  T
I  I  E  L  R  M  O  B  R  E  O  D  P  J  N  P  I  E  D  T
O  S  L  P  D  T  Y  I  Q  Q  J  C  M  V  E  V  U  E  S  R
```

Adolphus Busch	**Dale Carnegie**	**Kate Chopin**	**Sam Walton**	**Tennessee Williams**
Annie Malone	**Daniel Boone**	**Mark Twain**	**Scott Joplin**	**Walt Disney**
Charles Lindbergh	**Dred Scott**	**Marlin Perkins**	**Susan Blow**	
Charlie Parker	**Harry S Truman**	**Maya Angelou**		

MO TRIVIA

ANSWERS IN BACK

Q: What city is known as "the Gateway to the West"?

_____

Q: What is Missouri's nickname?

_____

Q: What handy dessert was introduced at the 1904 St. Louis World's Fair?

_____

Q: Samuel Clemens is known by what other name?

_____

Q: What Missouri politician started out as a farmer?

_____

Q: What is the name of the Maryland-to-California route of early settlers?

_____

Q: The first successful parachute jump from an airplane was made in 1912 in which city?

_____

Q: Which city has more fountains than any city except Rome?

_____

Q: What insect was declared Missouri's state insect?

_____

Q: What outlaw brothers were born in Kearney, Missouri?

_____

Q: What is mozarkite?

_____

Q: Missouri has an official state folk dance. What is it?

_____

Q: What is Missouri's first permanent settlement?

_____

Q: How many states border Missouri?

_____

Q: Name a drink introduced at the 1904 World's Fair.

_____

The committee of conference of
the Senate and of the House of Representatives on the subject of the disa-
greeing votes of the Two Houses, upon the
Bill entitled an "Act for the admission
of the State of Maine into the Union,"
Report the following Resolution.

Resolved.

1st. That they recommend to the
Senate to recede from their amendments
to the said Bill

2d. That, the two Houses agree to strike
out of the fourth section of the Bill from
the House of Representatives now pen-
ding in the Senate, entitled an "Act
to authorize the people of the Missouri
Territory to form a Constitution and State
Government and for the admission of
such State into the Union upon an equal
footing with the original States" The
following proviso in the following words,
and shall ordain and establish that
there shall be neither Slavery nor invol-
untary servitude

HISTORY AND MYSTERY

CHAPTER 6

A TORNADO RIPPED THROUGH JOPLIN IN 2011. IT'S ONE OF THE BIGGEST DISASTERS IN THE STATE'S MODERN HISTORY.

Winds estimated at more than two hundred miles per hour whipped through Joplin on May 22, 2011. The tornado sent vehicles flying and crushed entire neighborhoods. More than 150 people were found dead amidst the destruction. The tornado, estimated to be a mile wide, destroyed everything in a six-mile path.

FAMOUS AMERICAN OUTLAW JESSE JAMES IS FROM KEARNEY, MISSOURI.

Jesse James is one of Missouri's most famous outlaws. He was born in Kearney in 1847 and is known for his train and bank robberies. He led the James Gang for twenty years beginning during the Civil War. James was killed in 1882 by one of his own gang members. Today you can visit and tour the James farm, about thirty minutes outside Kansas City.

THE "CAVE STATE"

Caves are everywhere in Missouri. Some are part of Missouri's state parks and brewers in St. Louis have even used caves in their business of making beer. Some of the famous caves are Bridal Cave and Onondaga Cave.

LEMP MANSION AND BREWERY

The Lemp Mansion is part of St. Louis's mysterious fabric, and it's one of the best-known rumored haunted places in the city. John Adam Lemp arrived in St. Louis from Germany and established the Lemp Brewery. The mansion served as residence and brewery office. Its historic significance and the cellars in the basement have created mysterious rumors about the mansion.

Masons and Odd Fellows leave mysterious legends around the state.

Secret societies have left magnificent, historic buildings throughout the state. The Masonic Temple in St. Louis is a prominent landmark on Lindell Boulevard. The Masons, a fraternal organization, have put the temple up for sale in recent years. The Odd Fellows opened an entire compound north of Kansas City around 1900. The grounds included an orphanage and a nursing home to help care for relatives of its members. It was a working farm, and those who lived there grew most of what they ate. A cemetery is also on the property, and the site is now home to many mysterious stories and legends. Visitors say that ghosts live there. Ghost hunters have visited these "haunted" spots. People can even attend paranormal investigations at Belvoir Winery, which is now on the Odd Fellows property.

1803—THE LOUISIANA PURCHASE HELPED TO EXPAND THE UNITED STATES WESTWARD.

The United States purchased more than 820,000 square miles west of the Mississippi River from France in 1803. This was called the Louisiana Purchase, and the land that became Missouri was part of this purchase.

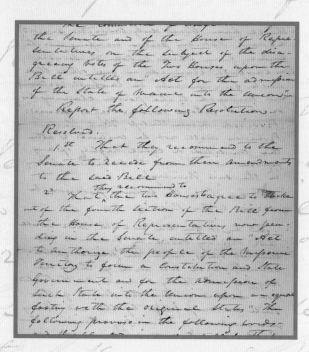

The Missouri Compromise allowed Missouri to join the United States as a slave state while Maine joined as a free state.

Missouri sought admission to the Union in 1819 as a slave state. But states were divided on the issue. As a compromise, Congress admitted Missouri as a state that could have slaves while at the same time admitting Maine as a free state, without slaves.

IN 1811–1812, FOUR OF THE BIGGEST EARTHQUAKES IN U.S. HISTORY HAPPENED IN NEW MADRID.

In 1811 and 1812, a series of earthquakes hit New Madrid in southern Missouri. They were so strong that people in New York and Washington, D.C., felt them. From December 1811 to March 1812, earthquakes rattled the middle of the country. At one point, the Mississippi River is said to have flowed backward.

THE FIRST FREE SCHOOL WEST OF THE MISSISSIPPI OPENED IN ST. CHARLES.

In 1818, a woman by the name of Rose Philippine Duchesne opened the first Sacred Heart school outside Europe. The school was called the Academy of the Sacred Heart and was the first free school west of the Mississippi. It opened in St. Charles. Her idea soon attracted more interest, and similar schools were opened across the Midwest.

1841—THE UNIVERSITY OF MISSOURI, THE FIRST STATE UNIVERSITY WEST OF THE MISSISSIPPI RIVER, OPENED ON APRIL 14.

The University of Missouri campus was built in Columbia because the people of Boone County came together to pledge money for land that would become the campus. The college opened in 1841, and it was the first state university west of the Mississippi. Creating the school was part of a state law that pushed for expanding education in Missouri. Mizzou, as it is called, became known for its studies of agricultural topics, and then the world's first journalism school was founded there in 1908.

1837—Missouri's first capitol in Jefferson City was destroyed by fire on November 15.

Missouri's current capitol is actually the third building in Jefferson City to serve as the location for Missouri lawmakers, because fire destroyed the first two buildings. A fire burned the capitol in 1837, soon after the state chose Jefferson City as its location. Then lightning struck the dome in 1911, which caused another fire resulting in the building of the capitol we know today.

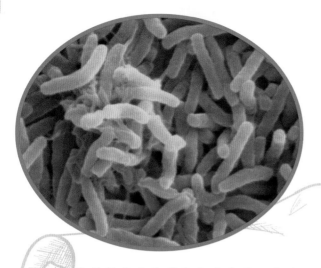

1849—CHOLERA EPIDEMIC STRUCK ST. LOUIS.

Cholera, a bacterial infection that is usually spread when human waste contaminates water, spread quickly in St. Louis in 1849. No one knows exactly how many people died from the disease, but physicians estimate that it could have been as many as seven or eight thousand.

ONE OF THE MOST IMPORTANT CASES WAS HEARD IN ST. LOUIS'S OLD COURTHOUSE IN 1857.

A slave named Dred Scott sued for his freedom, and the case was heard in St. Louis. He asked for freedom because he had lived in Illinois and Wisconsin Territory where there were no slaves. The Supreme Court ruled against him, and the outcry helped spark abolitionists' movement to outlaw slavery and helped to instigate the Civil War.

One of the first U.S. mail services started in St. Joseph.

The Pony Express was an important service when it came to getting news, mail, and letters from the eastern part of the United States to the western frontier. The service started in St. Joseph, Missouri, and went all the way to Sacramento, California. It was a total of 1,200 miles. Eventually, the trail was no longer needed, but today you can view some of its historic stops.

A GENERAL IN ST. LOUIS MADE A STATEMENT THAT SLAVES SHOULD BE FREE BEFORE ABRAHAM LINCOLN DID.

A year before the U.S. president made a formal order called the Emancipation Proclamation that freed the slaves in the U.S., a general in St. Louis had already done so. Major General John C. Frémont, who was commander of the Union's Western Department, issued a proclamation on August 30, 1861. It stated that anyone who took up arms against the United States would have property confiscated and that if they had slaves, the slaves would be "free men."

1865—MISSOURI WAS THE FIRST SLAVE STATE TO FREE SLAVES FOLLOWING U.S. PROCLAMATION.

In 1865, the United States abolished slavery with an ordinance calling for immediate emancipation. Missouri was the first slave state to free slaves. The state did so even before Congress adopted the Thirteenth Amendment to the Constitution, which outlawed slavery.

THE FIRST PUBLIC KINDERGARTEN WAS OPENED IN ST. LOUIS BY SUSAN BLOW.

Susan Blow helped set a trend across the nation when she opened the first public kindergarten in the St. Louis area. It was in September 1873 that Blow started a kindergarten class for young students at Des Peres School. The idea of educating youngsters through kindergarten eventually spread nationwide.

1904—St. Louis was the scene of the World's Fair, an international festival that celebrated the city at the time.

The Louisiana Purchase Exposition, the official name of the 1904 World's Fair, made St. Louis an international star. It also had a historic impact on the city and drew crowds for several months. The exposition showcased performances and exhibits from around the world. It featured cultural attractions from across the globe as well as carnival and circus-like exhibits with exotic animals.

1980—COURT-ORDERED DESEGREGATION BEGAN IN MISSOURI.

A state program called desegregation attempted to mix students from different races and backgrounds together to help with academic performance. A federal court demanded that students in the 1980s and 1990s be bused from the city into suburban school systems, and some suburban students were bused to city schools. But in 1999 the state of Missouri removed the court from supervising the program. In recent years these programs have dwindled.

1945—WINSTON CHURCHILL, FORMER PRIME MINISTER OF ENGLAND, DELIVERED HIS "IRON CURTAIN" SPEECH AT FULTON'S WESTMINSTER COLLEGE IN MARCH.

The beginning of a chilling relationship between the United States and the former Soviet Union has a Missouri connection. Former British prime minister Winston Churchill gave a speech, now known as the "Iron Curtain" speech, at Westminster College in Fulton in 1945. With President Harry Truman on stage with him, Churchill spoke of the rising world power of the United States and warned of the spread of communism.

SCIENCE AND TECHNOLOGY

CHAPTER 7

RESEARCHERS AT THE DONALD DANFORTH PLANT SCIENCE CENTER WORK WITH MORE THAN ONE HUNDRED SPECIES OF PLANTS IN ALMOST 48,000 SQUARE FEET OF GREENHOUSE SPACE.

Missouri's vast farmlands and history of agriculture make it a likely place for some of the more inventive agricultural techniques. The Donald Danforth Plant Science Center in St. Louis focuses on the science of studying plants so that food can be grown better.

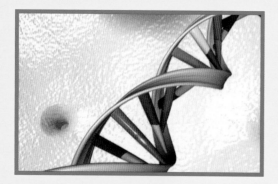

LABS AT WASHINGTON UNIVERSITY IN ST. LOUIS PLAYED A ROLE IN THE INTERNATIONAL SCIENCE PROJECT KNOWN AS THE HUMAN GENOME PROJECT.

Twenty years ago it seemed like science fiction—mapping all your genetic material, which determines everything from your height to your eye color—and having that information ready for doctors and researchers to use. But that's what happened when the McDonnell Genome Institute began its work in mapping the human genome. Now it's one of the top sequencing centers in the U.S. to use genomics to decode which genes are linked to which diseases.

A GYROSCOPE IS AN IMPORTANT TOOL TO MEASURE STABILITY AND TO HELP WITH NAVIGATION.

Charles Stark Draper grew up in Windsor, Missouri, and became an engineer, scientist, and teacher. But he is perhaps best known for inventing the gyroscope. It's a disk or wheel that spins on an axis and is used for stability and in navigation systems. They can be used to make gyrocompasses and can replace other compasses used for navigation.

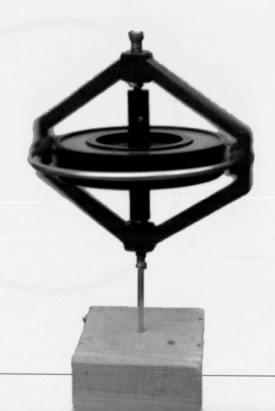

MISSOURI CAN EXPERIENCE CHANGES IN TEMPERATURE OFTEN BECAUSE OF ITS LOCATION IN THE MIDDLE OF THE COUNTRY, AWAY FROM THE COASTS.

Experts describe the climate in Missouri as continental marked by seasons. This means that the weather is usually cold and dry in the winter with hot summers. Weather can come from the northern plains and Canada and bring snowfall, rains, or humidity along the way. Missouri is flat, without mountains, and its temperature has frequent changes that are part of the seasonal climate. Temperatures rarely go above 100 degrees or below 0.

Buck's Ice Cream is an ice cream shop on campus produced by food science students at the University of Missouri.

The College of Agriculture, Food, and Natural Resources at the University of Missouri in Columbia is known for its focus on science about life and animals. Over the years students and researchers have worked on projects that helped improve the way farmers raise animals for food and helped them to farm better. Among the animal sciences research centers at the school are ones that focus on dairy, beef, swine, and equine. Researchers in labs there also alter genes of mice and rats to better understand diseases.

KANSAS CITY HAS BECOME A HUB FOR TECHNOLOGY COMPANIES LOOKING TO EXPERIMENT AND START UP.

Technology and latest innovation found its way to Kansas City in 2012 when Google chose the city for a program for superspeed Internet services called Google Fiber. Residents and businesses across the metro area signed up for the service that made it easier to surf and stream information from the Internet. In the last few years the company has been testing a service that would make the Internet fast and wireless.

Students at a state college in Rolla might find themselves working on a car that is powered by energy from the sun.

Future engineers of Missouri often go to Missouri University of Science and Technology in Rolla. Students there can become part of design teams for a solar car, a Mars rover, and other inventions while they are getting their engineering degree. Researchers at the school recently worked with a Greek university to show how to split water into hydrogen and oxygen in a more efficient and less costly way that could lead to using hydrogen as an energy source.

WOULDN'T IT BE COOL IF YOUR SCHOOL HAD A PLANETARIUM UNDER ITS ROOF? STUDENTS AT ROCK BRIDGE HIGH SCHOOL IN COLUMBIA DO.

Forget light pollution, when streetlights and human-made illumination make it difficult to see stars. And cloudy skies are no problem for the planetariums across the state. The St. Louis Science Center is home to the Zeiss Planetarium. Kansas City has Science City's Arvin Gottlieb Planetarium. The Southwest Missouri Planetarium is in Springfield. The Bushman Planetarium is in the northwestern part of the state. And students at Rock Bridge High School in Columbia have a planetarium on campus.

MICROCHIPS WERE AN IMPORTANT INVENTION THAT LED THE WAY TO TODAY'S SMARTPHONES, TABLETS, LAPTOPS, AND OTHER COMPUTING DEVICES.

Whether you call it a microelectronic circuit, an integrated circuit, or a chip, one of the inventors was Jack Kilby, who was born in Jefferson City. This invention was important because it laid the foundation for computers. He also came up with the technology for pocket calculators.

Take a Road Trip South of St. Louis to Visit the Original Bigfoot Monster Truck in Pacific.

As the story goes, Bob Chandler created the world's first monster truck—known for its huge wheels and 4x4 features—in south St. Louis. Now you can see the truck in a garage in Pacific. Like other huge trucks known as "Bigfoot," this truck was the heaviest, tallest, and widest pickup of its time. Other trucks and monster truck artifacts are on display for visitors at the Bigfoot 4x4 attraction.

LIQUID CRYSTALS ARE NOT MAGIC, BUT IT MAY SEEM LIKE THEY ARE. THEY ARE USED FOR INVENTIONS WE NOW TAKE FOR GRANTED.

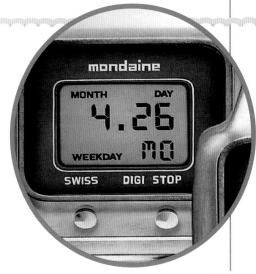

Inventor James Ferguson was born in Wakenda and became known for his groundbreaking work with liquid crystals, which led to LCD (liquid crystal display) watches and other inventions. He also found ways to use liquid crystals in mounted displays and other technology. We use LCD in small computers and notebooks.

SCIENCE MAZE

WEIRD MISSOURI FACTS

Blue Springs is home to the world's shortest St. Patrick's Day parade, which only goes across the street.

The world's first Segway track was built in Branson.

Hampshire Pet Products set the record for largest dog biscuit ever created in Joplin.

A peanut butter-banana pie sold for $3,100 in Rich Hill. Now THAT'S a sweet tooth!

During a food drive, the largest can pyramid ever was created in Kansas City, using 17,575 donated cans. Don't worry. All of the canned food was donated after the record was set.

The world's largest rooster is in Branson. He's forty-three feet high and stands outside the Great American Steak and Chicken House. I'd hate to have him wake me up in the morning.

There's a twelve-foot-long pecan in Brunswick, making it the world's largest. That's nuts!

In Richland diners can eat a meal at a restaurant inside a cave. It's called the Cave Restaurant and Resort. No bats allowed.

ANSWERS IN BACK OF BOOK

JUST EAT IT!

CHAPTER 8

Sugar Momma's in Hermann has more than fifty varieties of pie, including . . . bacon apple. "Let's just cut to the chase. Bacon makes everything better," they say.

Missouri State Fair Fare

SOME OF THE MOST POPULAR CONTESTS IN THE EARLY YEARS OF THE FAIR INCLUDED PIE EATING, CRACKER EATING, AND SAUSAGE EATING.

Folks have been flocking to Sedalia for more than 115 years to attend the annual Missouri State Fair. For a lot of visitors hitting the fair, it's all about the food. Love ice cream? You can get a scoop of Mizzou's own Tiger Stripe, made by students at the university. Or try honey-sweetened ice cream from the Missouri Bee Keepers Association. Fried foodstuffs are crowd-pleasers too, everything from classic corn dogs to cheese-on-a-stick. Fried sweets? Even better: sugary funnel cake and fried Oreos hit the spot. Finish up with some fruits and veggies, available at the giant fresh produce stand inside the Agriculture Building!

If you have a sweet tooth, Missouri is the state for you! From the very fancy chocolates (some that look more like jewels than food) at Christopher Elbow Artisanal Chocolates in Kansas City to the flash-frozen-before-your-eyes nitro ice cream at St. Louis's Ices Plain & Fancy, we've got a sugar rush. Try a banana split with Central Dairy's creamy ice cream in Jefferson City or the famous milkshakes at St. Louis's Crown Candy Kitchen *(they also make TONS of their own candies).*

It's called the Corner Store, but pop inside this Cape Girardeau shop to find homemade chocolates and rock candy. Chase Candy Company in St. Joseph can crank out 72,000 of their famous Cherry Mash candy bars a day. (They've been making them since 1876, so they've had a lot of practice.) In Phillipsburg, Redmon's Candy Factory has become a must-stop on the highway, for everything from fudge to gummies. Now, don't let the grown-ups see this, but there's another roadside stop in St. Robert that you kind of can't help but giggle at: Uranus Fudge Factory. And for a completely different kind of experience, check out the luxurious Chocolaterie Stam in Hannibal: it's the only Missouri location for this renowned Dutch confection maker.

Farm-to-Fork Food

Missouri has the second-highest number of farms of any state in the U.S.

Everything from sweet potatoes and gooseberries to beef and bacon is available from Missouri farmers.

How can you get a taste of your state's bounty? Try visiting a local farmers' market during the growing season: there are large and small ones in Springfield, Chillicothe, Kansas City, Maplewood, Moberly, Bolivar, Neosho, Ferguson, Webb City, Kirksville, Mountain Grove, Rolla, and many more. You'll often find the same people who grow the food, raise the chickens, and make the honey selling their products.

EATING LOCAL FOODS CAN save money (since it doesn't have to be transported a long way); taste better (since fruits, veggies, and meats can grow until right before they are sold and consumed); and be good for the economy (since the money you spend on it goes straight to a local resident).

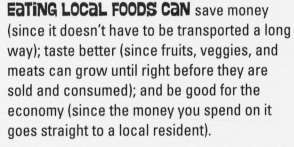

FARM-TO-TABLE RESTAURANTS like Green Dirt Farm in Weston, Bluestem in Kansas City, and Sycamore in Columbia try to get many of their menu items from local farmers, ranchers, and producers.

Drink It In

In the world before Big Soda, there were a lot more choices than just Coke or Pepsi. In Missouri, while some pops have passed, others are still produced and consumed here. In Independence, Polly's Soda Pop was the rage from 1923 to 1967. Now, a local couple has revived the business and begun bottling Polly's in flavors like pineapple and cream soda.

THE ORIGINAL NAME OF 7-UP WAS BIB-LABEL LITHIATED LEMON-LIME SODA.

Another Missourian, Charles Leiper Grigg of Price's Branch, was something of a pop prodigy: he invented Whistle, a popular orange soda, for the Vess company in St. Louis. He later invented what became 7-Up, an early contender in the lemon-lime flavor market.

IBC ROOT BEER was first brewed by St. Louis's Griesedieck family, who were known more for their beer. During Prohibition, when alcohol was outlawed, "soft" (non-alcoholic) drinks like root beer soared in popularity. Another St. Louis entry, Fitz's, traces its history to the 1940s; today, the brand includes root beer, cream soda, black cherry soda, key lime soda, ginger ale, and more. In Branson, Ozark Mountain Bottleworks churns out limited-edition butter beer, along with grape pop and Ozark Mountain lemonade.

The Greatest Hits of Grub

Classic Missouri foods are beloved (and occasionally trash-talked!) not just by locals but in some cases by people around the world. Have you tried these delicacies, which have roots right here?

- Gooey Butter Cake
- Toasted Ravioli
- Provel Cheese (found atop St. Louis–style pizza)
- Pork Steak
- Burnt Ends (and other KC-style BBQ)
- Slinger
- Waffle Ice Cream Cone
- Frozen Custard Concrete
- St. Paul Sandwich

FOOD FAVORITES often have a "born by accident" story behind them, like the tale of the toasted ravioli (cook accidentally drops an uncooked ravioli into a deep fryer!) and the waffle cone (cooked up by an ice-cream vendor and a waffle vendor who shared adjacent booths at the 1904 St. Louis World's Fair).

The Best Thing Since . . .

July 7, 1948. Just after Independence Day. What a perfect time to celebrate an American treasure: sliced bread! The Chillicothe Baking Company advertised it would begin that day selling Kleen Maid bread, sliced on the Rohwedder bread-slicing machine invented in Iowa. Obviously, the idea caught on (though it took a little while for consumers to adjust to a pre-sliced loaf). And today, Chillicothe celebrates its heritage with a museum displaying an antique bread-slicing machine, on loan from the Smithsonian Institution.

Eat This Truck

Taking fast food to the next level, the craze for food trucks continues to sweep the state. From organized weekly festivals in city parks to a "truck row" outside popular tourist areas, there's a time and a truck for just about every craving! Here are some of the ones that get our mouths watering:

- **Bochi (Kansas City):** fried rice-stuffed chicken wings
- **Easterly's Chuckwagon (Springfield):** a rustic covered wagon setup, with smoked turkey legs and other meat cooked over an open fire
- **Holy Crepe (St. Louis):** sweet and savory crepes stuffed with fruit, veggies, chocolate, or cheese
- **London Calling Pastry Company (Springfield):** pasties, or filled dough pockets, with everything from spicy chicken tikka masala to sausage and mashed potato
- **Lunch Box Truck (Carthage):** fresh salads, gourmet sandwiches, and soups
- **Plantain District (Kansas City):** Cuban specialties like ropa vieja and guava BBQ sliders
- **TacO the Town (Joplin):** wide variety of tacos, burritos, and nachos
- **Vincent Van Doughnut (St. Louis):** fresh, from-scratch doughnuts and kolache

Pancakes with a Past

You are lucky enough to live in such amazing times, you can have pancakes pretty much ANY time you want! And the history of how those hot, yummy pillows of deliciousness come right off the pan to your plate starts in St. Joseph. That's where, in 1889, a pair of local entrepreneurs bought a mill with the idea to package and sell a ready-mix, self-rising pancake flour.

The pancake mix, today owned by Quaker Oats, continues to be a global success.

Nancy Green, who was hired to portray the character of Aunt Jemima when the pancake mix was new, was a formerly enslaved African American woman who went on to become the first living trademark for a product. She promoted the brand from 1893 until her death in 1923.

Buckwheat cakes – with sausage! Um·m!

Make this wonderful old-time breakfast the easy Aunt Jemima way!

AUNT JEMIMA BUCKWHEAT FLOUR

Heads up! Throwed rolls incoming!

Hot bread math! The rolls at Lambert's are five inches in diameter; if all the rolls baked in one year were laid out side by side, it would equal 177.27 miles of rolls.

If you've driven the highways of the state, you've probably seen the billboards advertising Lambert's Cafe and its famous "throwed rolls." That's no typo: at the family-owned restaurant (the original is in Sikeston, with two others in Ozark and Foley, Alabama), roving waitstaff push along a big cart of fresh-baked dinner rolls and literally toss them over the heads in the dining room to anyone brave enough to stick a hand up in the air. Hot, yummy, and even better if you can wait long enough for the traveling bucket of sorghum molasses to come around too.

PEOPLE AND PLACES

CHAPTER 9

UNUSUAL TOWN NAMES

There are hundreds of cities, towns, villages, and municipalities in the state of Missouri. Some are major metro areas like St. Louis and Kansas City. Many are tiny with populations in the teens. But one thing is certainly true about Missouri towns: they sure have some strange names! When you scan the map, you see bizarre names: towns spelled like cities from other countries (but pronounced differently) and some that make you scratch your head. Here are a few of the more unusual ones and the stories behind them.

Plato, MO

Plato is a town in Texas County with a population of 109. It was named after the ancient Greek philosopher Plato and was designed as a city to be governed by "thinking men," like what was described in Plato's *Republic*. Plato is also the mean center of population distribution for the United States, meaning it is perfectly centered with Americans all around!

A post office in Novelty has been around since 1854.

Novelty is a unique town in many ways. The longtime trading post town lies in Knox County and was named by Dr. Pendry, who was known as a very eccentric man. The town name filing shows that he named the town on a whim for the assortment of merchandise that was in his store.

Tightwad, MO

Tightwad is a small town in Henry County with a population of 69. That wasn't the original name of the town, but according to official Missouri records, it was changed after an argument over money between a carpenter and the owner of a store.

THE ORIGINAL NAME OF TIGHTWAD WAS EDGEWOOD.

Creve Coeur, MO

THERE ARE CABINS STILL STANDING IN CREVE COEUR THAT DATE BACK TWO HUNDRED YEARS.

Creve Coeur is named after a broken heart. The suburb of St. Louis has a population of 17,833 and a rather large lake that is the reason for the legend and the name. Creve Coeur is French for heartbreak. Local legend has it that the lake "formed itself into a broken heart" when an Indian princess jumped from a cliff near the lake over the love of a French fur trapper.

Liberal, MO

THE TOWN'S NAME COMES FROM THE LIBERAL LEAGUE OF LAMAR, MISSOURI.

Liberal is a town in Barton County, which is actually one of the most conservative areas of the country. It was given the name by George Walser, as he foresaw the town as an atheist utopia that would have no churches or saloons. Walser claimed that "no person could live in a Christian community and express an honest opinion regarding Christian religion adverse to the interest of priestcraft without hazarding his business and social standing."

Licking, MO

Licking is one of those towns that gets a second glance every time you see the name. The name of the town in Texas County comes from a nearby buffalo salt lick that gave the area a significant deer population in the 1800s.

THE TOWN WAS FIRST NAMED BUFFALO LICK, OR SIMPLY THE LICK.

Olympian Village, MO

MANY OF THE STREETS ARE NAMED IN HONOR OF GREEK LEGENDS AND LOCATIONS, LIKE HERCULES PLACE, KRONOS DRIVE, AND PARTHENON DRIVE.

Olympian Village is a town in Jefferson County with a population of 761. Some think the name has a connection to the 1904 Olympics in St. Louis, but that's not true. The name comes from Greek culture.

Missouri history is one of Native American history. In fact, the two are so intertwined that the name Missouri actually comes from the Native American word "Missouria," which means "big canoe people." But the Missouria tribe is just one of several Native American groups that called Missouri their home before our state was a state.

Seven tribes called the region that would become Missouri home.

Chickasaw: This Native American tribe was found extensively throughout the southeastern United States and spread into southeast Missouri.

Illini: The Illini tribe, which is the namesake for the state of Illinois, also had a large presence in Missouri. The original name is actually Illiniwek, which means "the best people."

Ioway: This tribe was one of the smallest in Missouri, with only a limited presence along the border with Iowa. The Ioway actually had a different name for their tribe, Baoje, which means "gray snow."

Missouria and Otoe: The Missouria tribe is the namesake for the state of Missouri and had a large presence throughout much of central and west-central Missouri. These were the first Indian tribes to meet with Lewis and Clark, and they had good trade with frontiersmen from France, Spain, and other Americans.

Osage: The Osage tribe is one of the most well-known Native American groups that lived in the state of Missouri, and they are known as Missouri's indigenous people. Their lands spread from central Missouri all the way to Kansas and Arkansas.

Quapaw: The Quapaw held lands in southeast Missouri along the Arkansas border. In fact, they were also called "Akansea" meaning "land of the downriver people," which is where the name Arkansas is derived.

SEVERAL OTHER TRIBES ALSO HAD A SMALLER PRESENCE IN THE REGION

Cherokee	Sac and Fox
Delaware	Shawnee
Kickapoo	

MISSOURI'S HEALING SPRINGS

Fresh water is vital for good health. Before the days of drilling technology, fresh water was a key natural resource for development. That's the reason so many cities and towns grew around lakes, rivers, and springs. When the medicinal water fad was growing across the country in the late 1800s and early 1900s, springs became all the rage for health fanatics. So these natural sources of water became big business. Missouri's unique topography with numerous caves and abundant springs was perfectly poised to satisfy the needs of patrons seeking better health through the environment. Even today, these springs still attract millions of visitors a year to enjoy the natural beauty throughout Missouri.

El Dorado Springs

There isn't much to see any more with this western Missouri spring, but its water was once touted as a medicinal cure. Native Americans used to bring sick members of their community to this spring. But it wasn't until an Arkansas farmer's sick wife began to get well after drinking from the spring that interest in the area began to expand.

THE STONE RUINS STILL SIT ALONG THE RIVER FOR CANOEISTS TO SEE.

Welch Springs

THE HOSPITAL FAILED BECAUSE PEOPLE WERE UNABLE TO GET TO THE REMOTE LOCATION.

One of the lesser-known springs in the state of Missouri, this location along the Current River in Van Buren was thought to be a cure-all for the ills of society. A doctor from Illinois built the Welch Spring Hospital near the entrance to the cave where the spring came out. Dr. Christian Diehl envisioned a natural spa where visitors could enjoy the cool, pollen-free air from the cave and the natural water from the spring.

Excelsior Springs

THE SPRING WATER WAS REPORTED TO CURE TUBERCULOSIS.

This spring north of Kansas City became a travel destination as people flocked to the area to partake in the healing "medicinal" value of the water. The water around Excelsior Springs was reported to have cured several people of their ills, so a health spa and resort developed around the water source.

THE CITY HALL IS ALSO CALLED THE "HALL OF WATER."

Pertle Spring

This spring was so popular that it was once one of Missouri's largest attractions.

Many people in Warrensburg know this area as home to a nearby golf course and the University of Central Missouri, not realizing the amazing history surrounding the actual spring. The sulfur spring drew thousands of visitors to the area with the belief that the smelly, oddly colored water would heal them.

Loutre Lick

EARLY SETTLERS TRAVELED TO THIS AREA FOR RELIEF OF ILLNESSES.

The unusual name of this mineral spring about fifty miles west of St. Louis comes from a combination of the French word *loutre* (otter) and lick from a nearby salt lick in the river. The history of this area being used as a **healing spring dates back to Daniel Boone and Thomas Hart Benton.**

HAUNTED PLACES IN MISSOURI

Some people believe in ghosts, others are skeptical. So finding the most haunted places in Missouri can be a difficult task, because believers of the paranormal believe they know where the most haunted places are, while others will say there are no haunted locations. So the best way to go about ranking haunted sites is to see what the ghost hunters most often agree on. We studied many of their reports and lists and came up with what researchers feel must be included in any list of the most haunted places in Missouri.

Missouri State Penitentiary (Jefferson City, Missouri)

THE NICKNAME FOR THE STATE PEN IS THE "BLOODIEST 47 ACRES IN AMERICA."

Included on almost every list and named by most every ghost hunter, the Missouri State Penitentiary certainly ranks as one of the creepiest places in the state. The old prison in Jefferson City has been known to have an amazing amount of paranormal activity. The state pen housed some of the most dangerous criminals ever known.

Landers Theater (Springfield, Missouri)

REPORTS OF HEARING A BABY CRYING IS A LANDERS THEATER LEGEND.

This building is listed on the National Register of Historic Places but is also known among ghost hunters as a place with plenty of paranormal activity. The old Springfield Little Theater was damaged in a fire in 1920 in which a janitor lost his life. Some witnesses report seeing that janitor roaming the balcony.

Epperson House (Kansas City, Missouri)

The Epperson House was included on the TV show *Unsolved Mysteries* as one of the *Top 5 Haunted Houses in the United States.*

This building on the campus of the University of Missouri–Kansas City is on most every haunted list. It was a home formerly owned by Uriah Epperson. His daughter died in the home during construction, and witnesses say they still see her late at night wearing an evening gown.

Ravenswood Mansion (Bunceton)

SOME PEOPLE HAVE REPORTED THE MUSIC BOX SUDDENLY PLAYING AND LAUGHTER COMING FROM VARIOUS ROOMS AT NIGHT.

This is one of the most beautiful, yet creepy, historic mansions in Missouri. It was built for the Leonard family in the late 1800s, but some say they never left. The elder woman died in the home, which is when the reports of paranormal activity began. A servant tried to get into her bedroom shortly after her death but discovered that the door was locked from the inside. Upon further inspection, no one was inside the room, which would have made it impossible to lock.

Glore Psychiatric Museum (St. Joseph, Missouri)

NUMEROUS PSYCHIATRIC PATIENTS DIED THERE OVER THE YEARS, AND WITNESSES SAY THEY ARE STILL THERE LOOKING FOR A CURE TO THEIR MENTAL ILLNESS.

Any location that includes the words "lunatic asylum" is a good place to start looking for the unusual. The present-day museum was once Missouri State Lunatic Asylum Number 2. Reports are that the motion detectors often go off, even when no one is around. Others actually report seeing people walking the halls and hearing people screaming and asking for help.

Prosperity School Bed and Breakfast (Joplin, Missouri)

This old school was just an empty building for three decades, but some believe the children never left. The building has been converted into a bed and breakfast, and many of the guests say they still get the creeps at night. There are reports of kids still running up and down the halls, and the ghost of the school nurse has also been seen. Some guests even report the feeling that kids are crawling into bed with them at night.

THE TV SHOW *GHOST HUNTERS* CAPTURED WHAT THEY SAY IS A PICTURE OF THE KIDS IN THE HALLWAY.

OTHER GREAT SITES TO CHECK OUT FOR HAUNTINGS IN MISSOURI

Thespian Hall, Boonville

Hotel Bothwell, Sedalia

Hotel Savoy, Kansas City

Glenn House, Cape Girardeau

Pythian Castle, Springfield

The Haunted Tavern, Columbia

Jefferson Barracks and Cemetery, St. Louis

RELIGIONS IN MISSOURI

Religion has always had a big impact on life in Missouri. In fact, you can see it reflected in the names of the cities and counties across the state. Cities like St. Louis, St. Charles, St. Joseph, and others have religious derivations. The first Disciples of Christ Church that was built west of the Mississippi was built near Fayette before Missouri was even a state. The first Baptist church west of the Mississippi was built in Cape Girardeau County. And one part of our diverse religious history includes a story of a religion that wasn't welcome here. The Mormons settled near Independence but were forced out of the state by groups that didn't agree with their religious practices.

Currently, our state has a diverse background when it comes to religion. According to Pew researchers, 80 percent of all Missourians say they are affiliated with a religious group. The Southern Baptists have the largest population with nearly 750,000 members, followed by Catholics at 724,000 and Methodists at 226,000.

Christian: 77%
Non-Christian Religions: 3%
No Religion: 20%

RELIGION HAS ALWAYS HAD A BIG IMPACT ON LIFE IN MISSOURI.

IMMIGRANTS/ETHNIC GROUPS

Missouri, much like the United States itself, has always been a melting pot of people from around the globe. The Germans were the first group to come in large numbers, which is why so many of our cities have names from that area of Europe. According to the U.S. Census Bureau in 2000, an estimated 24 percent of Missourians trace their roots back to Germany, which is twice as much as any other group. Second is Irish ancestry with about 13 percent, followed by English.

You can still see the diverse backgrounds on display around the state, from German festivals in Hermann, to Italian sections of St. Louis like the Hill, the Sudanese neighborhoods in Kansas City, and the large Mexican population in southwest Missouri. In fact, in recent years Missouri has gotten even more diverse. Following the wars in the former Yugoslavia, many Bosnians found shelter in St. Louis. It's now estimated that there are seventy thousand people from Bosnia and Herzegovina living in St. Louis, which is the largest concentration of this group anywhere outside their home country.

MISSOURI NOW!

CHAPTER 10

GREAT GRAIN GODDESS! ATOP THE 260-FOOT-HIGH DOME, EAGLE-EYED VISITORS WILL SEE A BRONZE STATUE OF CERES, THE ROMAN GODDESS OF AGRICULTURE.

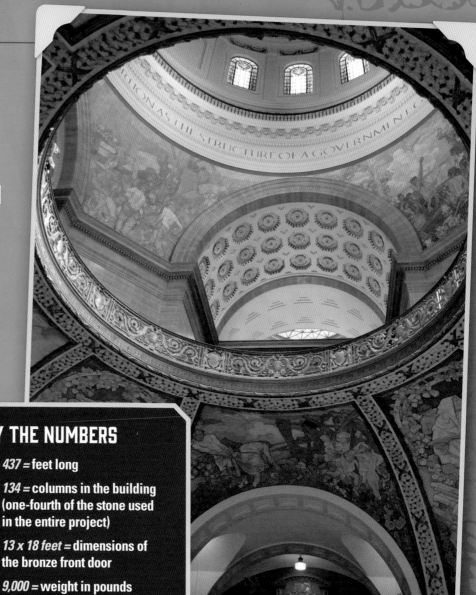

MISSOURI CAPITOL, BY THE NUMBERS

3 = number of acres the building occupies

69 = number of architecture firms who entered the design competition for the building

285 = concrete piers supporting the building

437 = feet long

134 = columns in the building (one-fourth of the stone used in the entire project)

13 x 18 feet = dimensions of the bronze front door

9,000 = weight in pounds of the bronze chandelier hanging in the dome

It was "Happy 100th birthday!" to the stately Missouri State Capitol in 2017 . . . although it's a little bit complicated. The massive, Roman Renaissance–style building, created from Carthage limestone, is actually the sixth structure to serve as the seat of state government. Previous capitols were located in St. Louis and St. Charles, but in 1826 it seemed to make sense to find a more central location to conduct the state's business. Two prior buildings in Jefferson City were destroyed by fires. In May 1913, ground was broken for the present capitol, which took more than four years to complete.

And if you find yourself in Jefferson City, make sure to check out the tours offered at the Missouri State Penitentiary (the state's historic jail), the Missouri Supreme Court, and the governor's mansion.

Libraries of the Future

Missouri libraries offer amazing programs and experiences that let you create, invent, collaborate, and learn. The scope is endless, from digital archives of historical artifacts to cutting edge technology. Visit your library to stretch the bounds of what's possible.

As much as we love our screens and digital devices, there will always be books. (You're holding one right now!) From digital downloads to community events, the library's traditional role of storing and making sense of information has moved into the modern era with ease.

The University City Public Library will check out a telescope for you to take home and stargaze. In Springfield, an heirloom seed library (at the public library) lets residents "check out" seeds for a wide variety of veggies and flowers. The St. Louis County Library system offers hands-on science kits for patrons to play with at home and also partners with the anti-racism organization WeStories to provide multicultural storybooks and family discussion ideas for young readers.

The St. Louis Public Library's Central branch houses the Creative Experience, a digital makerspace, plus a full recording studio for audio projects. Mid-Continent Public Library in Kansas City is developing a "story center," where digital, oral, and written stories will come together. The Nevada Public Library built its Next Level makerspace to give teens a place to tinker and collaborate with everything from textiles to stop-motion video software.

Nonprofit organizations can find a one-stop shop at the St. Louis Public Library's Grants & Foundation Center. The Kansas City Public Library's H&R Block Business and Career Center deals in every aspect of entrepreneurship. And having a card for just about any public library in the state is your ticket to free online classes, genealogy/family history databases, streaming music and video, and ebooks and audiobooks.

MO LOOKS BACK

200 YEARS AGO

First civil rights demonstration in the U.S. in 1819 at the courthouse in St. Louis, protesting the entry of Missouri into the Union as a slave state

100 YEARS AGO

Spanish influenza epidemic sweeps the nation, with St. Louis faring relatively better than other large cities (with a death rate of 358 per 100,000 residents), thanks in part to sweeping, citywide school and business closures; Urban League of St. Louis founded to address issues of concern to African Americans; Springfield teens build and govern the nation's first "city in miniature," Tiny Town, as part of a promotional campaign for the city's construction industry

75 YEARS AGO

An all–St. Louis baseball World Series, as the St. Louis Cardinals eventually prevail over the St. Louis Browns at Sportsman's Park; the film *Meet Me in St. Louis,* starring Judy Garland, is released, telling the story of a family in the year before the 1904 World's Fair; Cape Girardeau Regional Airport opens

50 YEARS AGO

St. Louis Cardinals attempt to defend their baseball World Series championship but ultimately fall to the Detroit Tigers; deadly riots sweep portions of Kansas City in the aftermath of the assassination of Dr. Martin Luther King Jr.; Arch Coal, the second-largest coal supplier in the U.S., founded in St. Louis; Metropolitan Community College founded in Kansas City

INNOVATE IN THE SHOW-ME STATE

When you think of the center of technological innovation, you think of California's famed Silicon Valley. But between Kansas City and St. Louis, an area known as Silicon Prairie is emerging. Companies like Square (a mobile payment system co-founded by Twitter founder Jack Dorsey), Microsoft, and Sprint, have a major presence in the area. And technology incubators, nonprofits, and investors—like T-REX, Kansas City Startup Village, Arch Grants, Kauffman Foundation, Cortex, Venture Cafe, and more—work hard to make the cities attractive places for new industries and startups to consider putting down roots.

KANSAS CITY (AND SURROUNDING SUBURBS) BEAT MORE THAN A THOUSAND OTHER APPLICANTS TO BE THE FIRST CITY CONNECTED BY GOOGLE FIBER, A FIBER-OPTIC NETWORK PROVIDING SOME OF THE FASTEST INTERNET CONNECTION SPEEDS IN THE COUNTRY.

Of course, start-ups aren't just technology companies. Entrepreneurship, the desire and drive to make something of your own, can happen in any field. So industries like fashion/design, food and beverage, and even education have people interested in pushing the envelope to create new products and ideas.

What if you're still in elementary school but have that urge to create? Consider finding your local makerspace or learning computer code. In St. Louis, the wildly colorful TechShop offers hands-on opportunities to use things like laser cutters, welding stations, 3D printers, and sewing machines to make the cool stuff in your head into real stuff in your hands. Across the state, KC's Hammerspace Community Workshop & Makerspace gives space and gear to those who want to play around with electronics, rocketry, blacksmithing, robotics, and more.

Blast off from Ferguson

In the suburb of St. Louis, the Challenger Center brings everyday people into contact with science, technology, engineering, and math issues that require teamwork and problem-solving skills to resolve. Missions available at the Ferguson site include "Voyage to Mars" and "Rendezvous with a Comet."

Show-Me Stars

Did you know you can see stars pretty much any night of the year in Missouri? We've picked some of the best viewing spots in towns around the state for you to check out on the next clear night!

Brommelsiek Park, Wentzville: meet up on clear Friday nights with helpful members of the Astronomical Society of Eastern Missouri, or come on your own anytime to the county park's dedicated astronomical viewing area.

St. Louis Science Center: First Friday events each month offer telescopes and spotting help from the St. Louis Astronomical Society, and there's always a view inside the planetarium.

Warkoczewski Observatory ("the Warko"), Kansas City: OK, what's cooler than a whole slew of large, fancy telescopes available to use for free on clear Friday nights, May through October? Well, they're on the roof. So you will be too.

Laws Observatory, Columbia: atop the University of Missouri Physics Building, Wednesday nights are taken over by the Central Missouri Astronomical Association, which hosts free public viewings.

Baker Observatory, north of Marshfield: Missouri State University hosts periodic viewing events that are free to the public.

Truman State University Observatory, Kirksville: set away from bright lights at the University Farm, it's home to twice-monthly public viewing nights.

ONE OF ONLY FOUR COMMUNITY-OWNED OBSERVATORIES IN THE UNITED STATES, THE STILABOWER PUBLIC OBSERVATORY IS ON THE CAMPUS OF LAMAR HIGH SCHOOL.

Astronomical Events Worth Watching

In addition to the nightly show happening overhead, there are a few extra-special upcoming events you might want to get your family together for at your *nearest stargazing spot*. Near the end of January of 2018 and 2019, Missourians can view a total lunar eclipse.

Ever heard the phrase "once in a blue moon," meaning something that happens rarely? *The seasonal blue moon* refers to an extra full moon that occurs within one season. So if instead of three full moons in winter, a year brings along four full moons in a winter, the third of the four is called a "blue moon." They tend to come along just once every few years: the next one visible here will be on May 18, 2019.

And mark November 11, 2019, for a really rare treat: *the planet Mercury glides directly in front of the sun* in what's called a "transit." This event comes around only about thirteen times every hundred years: the next one won't be until 2032! Why so uncommon? Because the Sun, Earth, and Mercury all have to be directly lined up—and the orbits of Earth and Mercury diverge by about seven degrees. They only catch up with each other periodically.

PLANES, TRAINS, AND AUTOMOBILES

CHAPTER 11

TROLLEY CARS WERE ALL THE RAGE IN THE LATE NINETEENTH AND EARLY TWENTIETH CENTURY.

In fact, St. Louis and Kansas City were leaders in this early form of mass transportation. They fell out of favor as more people bought cars and moved further from city centers, but streetcars are now seeing a renaissance across the country.

At one point, more than eight hundred cities had some sort of streetcar system, but that number had dwindled to only six at the lowest point. But as of 2012, more than forty cities have begun putting trolley cars back in place.

Kansas City: The KC street-car system opened in 2016 and has already proven to be very popular in downtown Kansas City. This streetcar runs over two miles of tracks throughout downtown and allows people to get off at sixteen different stops.

St. Louis: Streetcars used to line downtown St. Louis in the 1900s but fell out of favor just like in other major cities. In 2017, the 2.2-mile Loop Trolley is opening to connect "the Loop" area of University City to Forest Park in the city of St. Louis.

Springfield: Springfield also had a popular streetcar system in the early 1900s. The cars stopped running in the 1930s.

THE BRANSON AIRPORT IS THE ONLY PRIVATELY OWNED AND OPERATED COMMERCIAL AIRPORT IN THE ENTIRE UNITED STATES.

When most people think of going to the airport in Missouri, they likely think of St. Louis–Lambert International, Kansas City International, or the Springfield-Branson National Airport. But the number of airports across the state may surprise you!

The busiest airport in Missouri is in St. Louis. St. Louis–Lambert International Airport has the FAA code "STL." More than 6,200,000 people board airplanes each and every year through the gates at Lambert.

Kansas City International Airport ("MCI") is the second-busiest airport. Nearly 5,000,000 fly out of that airport on an annual basis. The strange three-letter FAA identifier dates back to when the airport was known at Mid-Continent International Airport.

The Springfield-Branson National Airport ("SGF") is the only other airport in Missouri that boards more than 100,000 people per year, with 368,000 fliers in 2016.

There are more than one hundred airports spread across the Show-Me State, handling massive jets, small propeller airplanes, and even seaplanes!

MORE THAN 6,200,000 PEOPLE BOARD AIRPLANES EACH AND EVERY YEAR THROUGH THE GATES AT LAMBERT.

MiSSOURi HaS NEaRLY TWO DOZEN iNTERSTATE HiGHWaYS.

Many people may not realize this, but Missouri is home to many historical sites when it comes to the interstate highway system. The official name of our interstate system is the Dwight D. Eisenhower National System of Interstate and Defense Highways. They were developed in the 1950s, but this effort goes back to 1916 when national leaders wanted to develop a system to get around the country easier. Currently, Missouri has the sixth-largest highway system in the nation.

Missouri is one of three states that lays claim to having the starting point of the interstate highway system. This dates back to August 2, 1956, when a contract was signed to fix up the aging Route 66 (now Interstate 44). But on August 13, 1956, another contract was awarded and work began in St. Charles County on what later became Interstate 70.

Missouri's history with Route 66 is also legendary. The "Mother Road" carved its way across sections of Missouri and was even mentioned in songs. Many parts of Route 66 are now gone, but long stretches remain from St. Louis, down to Waynesville, and on through Springfield and Joplin.

HISTORIC
MISSOURI
US
66
ROUTE

ODD NUMBERS FOR INTERSTATES RUN NORTH AND SOUTH, AND EVEN NUMBERS RUN EAST AND WEST.

STEALTH BOMBERS TRAVEL AT ONE THOUSAND FEET PER SECOND, JUST BELOW THE SPEED OF SOUND.

One of the most advanced aircraft in the history of the U.S. military calls an Air Force base in central Missouri its home. The stealth bomber is unique in that it can practically hide in the air despite its enormous size. Each of these massive jets cost more than $737 million when they were produced in the 1990s. That means a stealth jet of this caliber today would cost upwards of $1 billion each!

The secret flying machines were manufactured by Northrop Grumman, but only twenty-one were ever built. It certainly wasn't easy building a top secret jet when you are talking about something of this size and cost. But the U.S. military needed something to replace the aging B-52 bombers that could also carry nuclear weapons and fly across the globe undetected. It took more than ten years to complete, but when the stealth aircraft were done, they were truly revolutionary. That means overseas military missions can be accomplished after launching from Whiteman Air Force Base near Sedalia.

- *They are designed more like a horseshoe than a typical jet, which helps keep them invisible to radar.*

- *The engine is designed to be deep inside the jet so it doesn't put out much exhaust, while also keeping it cool so it doesn't stand out on radar.*

- *Stealth bombers travel at one thousand feet per second, just below the speed of sound.*

- *They can fly twelve thousand miles at a time with only one refueling needed mid-air.*

- *Each is 172 feet wide, which is more than half the length of a football field!*

Missouri plates were first designed so that every car would have the initials of the vehicle's owner!

Missouri has a long and storied history with motor vehicles. In fact, Missouri was one of the early states in adopting license plates for cars. The first plates in Missouri date back to 1911, only ten years behind the very first state, New York, to require motor vehicles to be registered with the state.

The format and color scheme in Missouri changed over the years. For the first thirty-seven years of license plate existence in Missouri (1911–1948), a new plate was designed every year. It wasn't until around 1950 that stickers began to be put on the plates so officials would know if they were expired. In 1976, the United States bicentennial logo was added. The Show-Me State slogan wasn't added until 1980.

Missouri will get new license plates again in 2019, just in time for the 2021 Missouri bicentennial. The new design will showcase Missouri's two hundredth year as a state. At that point, Missouri may also be a "one license plate" state.

- *Many universities and nonprofit organizations have also gotten on board with designing license plates.*

- *Nineteen states currently only require a single license plate, whereas Missouri requires one on the front and rear of the car.*

AUTOMOBILE MANUFACTURING HAS BEEN A BIG PART OF THE MISSOURI ECONOMY FOR THE PAST HUNDRED YEARS.

Some of the most iconic vehicles of all time were built at plants in Missouri, although many of these plants have now shut down. But there are still tens of thousands of people employed in the auto industry in the Show-Me State, producing hundreds of thousands of vehicles per year.

There are currently two major auto manufacturing plants operating in Missouri. In Wentzville, General Motors operates a factory where the Chevrolet Colorado, Chevrolet Express, GMC Canyon, and GMC Savana are currently produced. GM's full-size vans are also produced at this facility.

VEHICLES THAT WERE PRODUCED IN MISSOURI

- *Aerostar (Ford)*
- *Corvette (Chevrolet)*
- *Dorris (Dorris Motor Car Company)*
- *Explorer (Ford)*
- *Kansas City Touring Car (Kansas City Motor Car Company)*
- *LTD Crown Victoria (Ford)*
- *Nova (Chevrolet)*

In the Kansas City area, Ford operates a manufacturing plant in Claycomo. This is one of the busiest automotive factories in the world, producing the Ford F150 and Ford Transit. In fact, more vehicles are produced at this plant than any other in the United States.

Missouri was formerly home to major manufacturing plants in Hazelwood (Ford), Fenton (Chrysler), St. Louis (Chevrolet and Dorris), and Kansas City (Kansas City Motor Car and Leeds/General Motors).

1907

THE GREATEST OF ALL AMERICAN CARS

Coast to Coast Representation

The Dorris
"Built Up to a Standard, Not Down to a Price"

Centers of Distribution

EASTERN

ATLANTA	Bregmen Motors Company	Georgia, Alabama, S. Carolina, Florida
BOSTON	Guerin-de Redemont Co.	New England States, except Connecticut
NEW YORK	Corliss Motors Corporation	Greater New York, Connecticut, Northern New Jersey
PHILADELPHIA	J. Harry Schumacher & Co.	Eastern Pennsylvania, Southern New Jersey, Northern Delaware

CENTRAL

CHICAGO	Dorris Chicago Company	Northern Illinois
CINCINNATI	The Aslin Motor Car Co.	Southwestern Ohio
COLUMBUS	Evans-Ogden Motor Car Co.	Southern Ohio, except Cincinnati
FORT WORTH	Elliott, Ray & Bailey	Texas, Louisiana
KANSAS CITY	Stubbs Motor Company	Western Missouri, Kansas
MEMPHIS	West Tennessee Motor Co.	Western Tennessee
OKLAHOMA CITY	Hargrave-Parks Motor Co.	Oklahoma
ST. LOUIS	Weber Implement & Auto Co.	Eastern Missouri, Southern Illinois

WESTERN

LOS ANGELES	Albert J. Russell	Southern California, Arizona
SAN FRANCISCO	H. A. Seller Company	Northern California

High Grade Distributors and Dealers in open territory should investigate Dorris Passenger Cars and Trucks at the Shows

DORRIS MOTOR CAR CO., ST. LOUIS

TRAINS ACROSS MISSOURI

Missouri's central location is a big asset when it comes to transportation. And that's especially true for train transportation. Missouri is one of only a handful of states that provides access to both east and west coasts and has the third most railcars of any state operating on the rails. Even though train transportation has had its up and downs, rail traffic is expected to grow dramatically over the next few decades as more goods need to be moved more efficiently.

Two of the busiest rail terminals in the country are located in St. Louis and Kansas City. And many of the towns across the state were developed due to rail stops nearby. There are still four thousand miles of track in operation throughout the state!

The largest train carriers that operate rail lines in Missouri include Burlington Northern Santa Fe, CSX, Kansas City Southern, Norfolk Southern, and Union Pacific. Amtrak trains also still operate across the state, taking passengers along routes with spectacular views and twelve unique stopping points.

The goods crisscrossing the state on railcars vary greatly. Many of the cars you see are carrying bulk freight, such as coal and grain. Other times you see giant containers of goods that are placed on flatbed train cars. In many of these containers are everyday items that you would see in grocery stores and other retail stores. Other unique types of railcars allow trains to transport dozens of vehicles at one time. In fact, nearly 40 percent off all consumer goods (by tonnage) are moved by train at some point during their journey.

RAILROADS BEGAN OPERATING IN MISSOURI IN THE **1850s.**

MORE THAN 362,000 PEOPLE RODE AMTRAK TRAINS IN MISSOURI LAST YEAR.

MISSOURI IS RANKED FOURTH IN TONS OF GOODS CARRIED VIA RAIL.

Museum of Transportation

MORE THAN ONE HUNDRED VEHICLES ARE SHOWCASED, INCLUDING RARE VEHICLES THAT AREN'T USUALLY SEEN ON THE ROADS.

Transportation has been a major part of Missouri history since the state was founded in 1821. The growth of Missouri can be directly attributed to more effective ways of transportation, such as rail and vehicle. And transportation has certainly been a major economic force for the Show-Me State, from auto manufacturing, to the train/rail economy, and even airplane manufacturing. So it only makes sense that a museum dedicated to transportation would be located in Missouri.

The Museum of Transportation, located in suburban St. Louis, dates back to 1944. This facility in Kirkwood preserves and showcases the history of how Americans have used (and developed) transportation as our nation grew. The museum has one of the largest collections of transportation vehicles in the world on display.

In addition to the rare and unique train engines and vehicles on display, several other interesting types of transportation are also showcased. That includes two historic airplanes, buses, streetcars, and a towboat, to name a few.

MORE THAN SEVENTY LOCOMOTIVES ARE ON DISPLAY AT THE MUSEUM.

THE LAND WHERE THE MUSEUM IS LOCATED HAS ONE OF THE FIRST TRAIN TUNNELS BUILT WEST OF THE MISSISSIPPI RIVER.

650 WSM GRAND OLE OPRY WWW.OPRY.COM

SPORTS AND ENTERTAINMENT

CHAPTER 12

Musicians from the Show-Me State

Chuck Berry

CHUCK BERRY ATTENDED ST. LOUIS'S SUMNER HIGH SCHOOL.

RECORDED MORE THAN 30 TOP HITS!

Chuck Berry was one of the most influential musicians of our generation. The St. Louis native was the first person inducted into the Rock and Roll Hall of Fame, and he is a member of the Songwriters Hall of Fame.

Nelly

NELLY RECEIVED A STAR ON THE ST. LOUIS WALK OF FAME IN 2005, THE YOUNGEST PERSON TO GET THE HONOR.

Cornell "Nelly" Haynes Jr. has redefined the musical industry over the past decade. Nelly debuted to a national audience in 2000 with the album *Country Grammar* and quickly rocketed to the top of the charts numerous times.

PERFORMED AT THE SUPER BOWL HALFTIME SHOW WITH BRITNEY SPEARS

THE NAME "BIRD" CAME EITHER FROM HIM BEING "FREE AS A BIRD" OR THAT HE ACTUALLY HIT A BIRD WHILE DRIVING THE TOUR VAN.

Charlie Parker

CHARLIE PARKER WON NUMEROUS GRAMMYS, INCLUDING MANY AFTER HIS DEATH.

Charlie "Bird" Parker was a saxophonist from Kansas City who developed bebop. He may not have the name recognition of many of the Grammy winners of his time, but his influence on jazz is unmistakable.

HE AND DOLLY PARTON HAD MORE THAN A DOZEN NO. 1 HITS TOGETHER.

Porter Wagoner

Porter Wagoner is a legend of country music, selling millions of albums and staying true to his humble roots. The native of West Plains had dozens of hits throughout his career, especially when paired up with Dolly Parton.

Sara Evans

PEOPLE MAGAZINE NAMED HER ONE OF THE WORLD'S MOST BEAUTIFUL PEOPLE.

New Franklin native Sara Evans proved that a small-town Missouri girl can dominate the music industry. In the early years of this century, she received four straight nominations for Female Vocalist of the Year.

Sheryl Crow

"IF IT MAKES YOU HAPPY" WAS ORIGINALLY WRITTEN AS A COUNTRY SONG.

Sheryl Crow started her career as a school music teacher and singing backup for legends like Eric Clapton, Sting, and Michael Jackson. The Kennett native landed her own success with the release of the *Tuesday Night Music Club* album.

SHE WAS BRIEFLY ENGAGED TO TOUR DE FRANCE CHAMPION LANCE ARMSTRONG.

GIBSON, THE FAMOUS GUITAR MANUFACTURER, MAKES A SHERYL CROW SIGNATURE EDITION GUITAR.

ACTORS FROM THE SHOW-ME STATE

Missouri may be a long way from Hollywood, but the Show-Me State has certainly made its mark on the motion picture industry. Arguably, some of the most famous actors of all time grew up in Missouri and got their start on stages across the state. The theories about why Missourians have had so much success in motion pictures vary, but the fact remains that people from this state in the middle of the country have the ability to entertain the masses around the world.

Betty Grable

BETTY GRABLE WAS LISTED AS ONE OF THE TOP 10 BOX OFFICE STARS FOR TWELVE YEARS.

IN 1943, TWENTIETH CENTURY FOX HAD BETTY'S LEGS INSURED WITH LLOYD'S OF LONDON FOR A RECORD $1.25 MILLION.

The St. Louis native is famous for her work on the big screen and for her images that lifted the spirits of soldiers in World War II. She was in such high demand in the peak of her career that she was the highest-earning American woman in 1946–1947.

Brad Pitt

BRAD PITT IS A GRADUATE OF KICKAPOO HIGH SCHOOL.

By some estimates, the Springfield native is one of the most popular and highest-paid entertainers in history. He has been named *People* magazine's Sexiest Man Alive twice and continues to be one of the most "in demand" actors in the world.

Josephine Baker

MORE THAN TWENTY THOUSAND PEOPLE LINED THE STREETS FOR HER FUNERAL.

Known as the "Black Venus," Josephine Baker became one of the biggest international stars of the early and mid-1900s. Her fame in Europe exceeded her notoriety in the United States, and her fight for human rights was as much a part of her identity as her entertainment career.

REFUSED TO PERFORM IN CLUBS THAT WERE SEGREGATED.

WAS EXPELLED FROM CARNEGIE MELLON UNIVERSITY FOR RIDING HIS MOTORCYCLE THROUGH THE COLLEGE OF FINE ARTS BUILDING!

Steve McQueen

During his career, he was one of the highest-paid actors in Hollywood.

"The King of Cool," "The Bandito," and "The Rebel Legend" are all terms used to describe the man known for his great films and wild antics. McQueen was ranked No. 30 in *Empire* magazine's "Top 100 Movie Stars of All Time" list.

SPENT MUCH OF HIS CHILDHOOD IN SLATER, MISSOURI.

John Elroy Sanford (Redd Foxx)

SANFORD WAS THE ONLY ARTIST INVITED TO ELVIS PRESLEY'S WEDDING.

This native St. Louisan is one of the best-known comedians and actors of the late twentieth century. Fox is one of the small number of performers to have had the lead role in a television show on each of the big three networks.

HIS CHARACTER, FRED SANFORD ON *SANFORD AND SON*, WAS RANKED NO. 42 IN *TV GUIDE*'S LIST OF THE "50 GREATEST TV DADS OF ALL TIME."

Jean Harlow

SHE WAS RANKED NO. 22 ON THE AMERICAN FILM INSTITUTE'S "100 YEARS, 100 LEGENDS" LIST.

DIED AT THE AGE OF TWENTY-SIX.

The Kansas City girl was the original blonde bombshell, famous for movies and her ability to make front-page news of Hollywood magazines. "The Platinum Blonde" even appeared on the cover of *Life* magazine in 1937, making her the first actress to receive that honor.

MISSOURI IN THE MOVIES

Missouri has a long history on the big screen, with major movies being shot or set in the Show-Me State. In some instances, Missouri was prominently displayed as a part of the storyline. In other cases, our state was the backdrop for movies that represented other cities and countries. Part of the reason so many movies have been shot here is our unique cities and terrain. A large number of producers, writers, and actors also have called Missouri home over the years, and they push for movies to be shot here to showcase their home state.

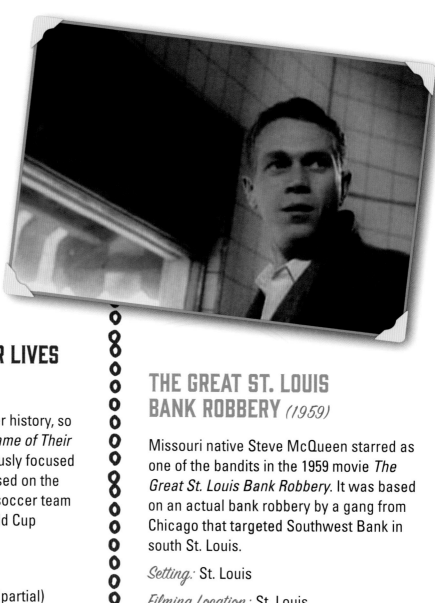

THE GAME OF THEIR LIVES

(2005)

St. Louis has a great soccer history, so when production of *The Game of Their Lives* began, the film obviously focused on Missouri. The film is based on the true story of the 1950 U.S. soccer team that beat England in a World Cup soccer match in Brazil.

Setting: The Hill (St. Louis)

Filming Location: St. Louis (partial)

THE GREAT ST. LOUIS BANK ROBBERY *(1959)*

Missouri native Steve McQueen starred as one of the bandits in the 1959 movie *The Great St. Louis Bank Robbery*. It was based on an actual bank robbery by a gang from Chicago that targeted Southwest Bank in south St. Louis.

Setting: St. Louis

Filming Location: St. Louis

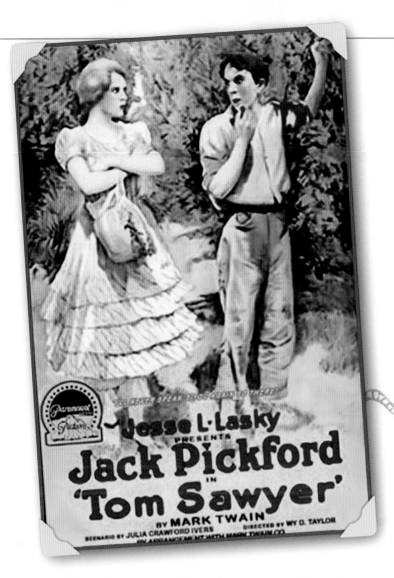

MEET ME IN ST. LOUIS (1944)

The quintessential St. Louis movie profiling a wonderful time in the city's history. *Meet Me in St. Louis* is the story of a St. Louis family and the anticipation leading up to the 1904 World's Fair. The film is on the "All Time 100 Best Films" list on Time.com.

Setting: St. Louis

TOM SAWYER (1973) AND HUCKLEBERRY FINN (1974)

Two of the most famous books and screenplays in literary history were based in areas around Missouri and shot in numerous locations across the state. Of course Mark Twain is the author of the books, so it makes sense that the settings are near to the heart of the famous playwright.

Setting: Along the Mississippi River

Filming Location: Arrow Rock, Lupus

PARENTHOOD (1989)

Steve Martin starred in this movie based on a family in St. Louis dealing with all the pressures of family life. Even though much of the filming was done in the Orlando area, the producers did their best to make it look like Missouri.

Setting: St. Louis centered

Filming Location: Lambert Airport (partial)

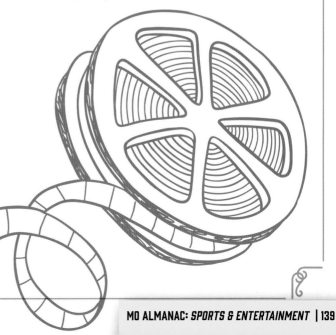

MISSOURI'S PRO TEAMS OF YESTERYEAR

Missouri has long been known for its outstanding professional sports teams. The St. Louis Cardinals are one of the most successful franchises in the history of Major League Baseball, and the Kansas City Royals have had a lot of recent success. And who could ever forget the I-70 Series between the two Missouri teams. The Kansas City Chiefs played in the first Super Bowl, and the St. Louis Rams made history with "The Greatest Show on Turf." But as is the nature of professional sports, some of our teams have moved on, leaving us with only great memories.

MLB

- The St. Louis Browns came to town in 1902 from Milwaukee, where they were known as the Brewers. The Browns moved to Baltimore in 1954 and became the Orioles.

- In 1968, the Kansas City Athletics headed west to Oakland to become the Oakland A's.

- The Kansas City Monarchs are a team that many people may not know of, but they have a significant part of the history of professional baseball. The team played in the Negro Leagues from 1920 to 1965. In fact, the Monarchs were the longest-running franchise in that league's history.

NBA

- The St. Louis Hawks were once the toast of St. Louis. But the team moved to Atlanta in 1968 after the owners sold the team to some buyers from Georgia.

- The Kansas City Kings moved to California in 1985 to become the Sacramento Kings. The Kings began playing in Kansas City in 1972 after moving from Cincinnati.

NFL

- St. Louis's history with the NFL goes back to 1960 when the Chicago Cardinals moved to the Gateway City. The Cardinals played in St. Louis for twenty-eight years before moving to Phoenix in 1988.

- The Los Angeles Rams moved to St. Louis in 1995, where they made two Super Bowl appearances and won the Super Bowl with one of the greatest teams of all time. The Rams moved back to LA in 2016.

NHL

- The Kansas City Scouts played their first game in 1974. But after two seasons, the team relocated to Denver to become the Colorado Rockies.

HORSESHOE PITCHING DATES BACK TO THE ROMAN EMPIRE.

Missouri is known for its professional sports teams and athletes, but few may realize that the Horseshoe Hall of Fame is located in Missouri. The idea to establish a hall of fame started in 1965, despite the sport being played for thousands of years. The decision to locate the hall of fame in Wentzville occurred in 2005. It took two more years for the facility to be built in Quail Ridge Park, but it now draws fans from around the world. The facility is situated on several acres of park land and has sixteen indoor and eight outdoor pitching courts.

MORE THAN FIFTEEN MILLION PEOPLE PITCH HORSESHOES IN NORTH AMERICA ALONE.

ANOTHER MISSOURIAN, PHOG ALLEN, IS CONSIDERED THE "FATHER OF BASKETBALL COACHING" AND WAS IN THE FIRST HALL OF FAME CLASS.

The inventor of basketball, James Naismith, coached at the University of Kansas, which is a short drive away from the College Basketball Experience.

There are few places in the United States that have a bigger history of college basketball than the Kansas City area. From legendary players to amazing tournament games in the area venues, Kansas City has made a huge imprint on college basketball. And the College Basketball Experience is now a part of that evolving history. In fact, Kansas City was the home of the NCAA for more than fifty years.

So when it came time to build the National Collegiate Basketball Hall of Fame, it only made sense that Kansas City would be its home inside the College Basketball Experience at the Sprint Center in 2007. The first hall of fame class was picked in 2006, and the hall continues to honor the greatest college basketball players on an annual basis.

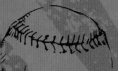

MISSOURIANS IN THE PROS

MISSOURIANS CURRENTLY IN THE MLB (2017)

Albert Pujols – LA Angels (Fort Osage)

Cody Asche – Chicago White Sox (Ft. Zumwalt West)

David Freese – Pittsburgh Pirates (Lafayette/Mizzou/SLCC-Meramec)

David Phelps – Miami Marlins (Hazelwood West)

Jacob Turner – Washington Nationals (Westminster Christian)

Josh Outman – Washington Nationals (Lindbergh/Central Missouri)

Lucas Harrell – Toronto Blue Jays (Ozark)

Max Sherzer – Washington Nationals (Parkway Central/Mizzou)

Nick Tepesch – Minnesota Twins (Blue Springs/Mizzou)

Ross Detwiler – Oakland Athletics (Wentzville/MSU)

Scott Van Slyke – LA Dodgers (John Burroughs)

Shae Simmons – Seattle Mariners (Scott City/SEMO)

Tom Layne – NY Yankees (Ft. Zumwalt South)

Trevor Rosenthal – St. Louis Cardinals (Lee's Summit West)

MISSOURIANS IN THE NBA (2017)

Alec Burks – Utah Jazz (Grandview)

Anthony Tolliver – Sacramento Kings (Kickapoo)

Ben McLemore – Sacramento Kings (St. Louis, Missouri)

Bradley Beal – Washington Wizards (Chaminade)

Brandon Rush – Minnesota Timberwolves (Westport)

David Lee – San Antonio Spurs (Chaminade)

Otto Porter Jr. – Washington Wizards (Scott City, Missouri)

Tyler Hansbrough – Charlotte Hornets (Poplar Bluff)

MISSOURIANS IN THE NHL (2017)

Ben Bishop – LA Kings (Chaminade)

Brandon Bollig – Calgary Flames (Francis Howell North)

Chris Wideman – Ottawa Senators (Chaminade)

Joe Vitale – Detroit Red Wings (CBC)

Paul Stastny – St. Louis Blues (Chaminade)

MISSOURIANS IN THE NFL (2016–2017)

Adrian Clayborn – Atlanta Falcons (Webster Groves)

Aldon Smith – Oakland Raiders (Raytown/Mizzou)

Allen Barbre – Philadelphia Eagles (East Newton/Missouri Southern)

Beau Brinkley – Tennessee Titans (Kearney/Mizzou)

Blaine Gabbert – Jacksonville Jaguars (Parkway West/Mizzou)

Brandon Williams – Baltimore Ravens (Rockwood Summit/Missouri Southern)

C. J. Mosley – Detroit Lions (Waynesville/Mizzou)

Chase Coffman – Free Agent (Raymore-Peculiar/Mizzou)

Christian Kirksey – Cleveland Browns (Hazelwood East)

David Bass – Tennessee Titans (University City/Missouri Western)

Donald Stephenson – Denver Broncos (Blue Springs)

E. J. Gaines – LA Rams (Ft. Osage/Mizzou)

Ezekiel Elliott – Dallas Cowboys (John Burroughs)

Jairus Byrd – New Orleans Saints (Clayton)

Jeremy Maclin – Kansas City Chiefs (Kirkwood/Mizzou)

Justin Britt – Seattle Seahawks (Lebanon/Mizzou)

Kony Ealy – Carolina Panthers (New Madrid County Central/Mizzou)

Maurice Alexander – LA Rams (Eureka)

Sheldon Richardson – New York Jets (Gateway/Mizzou)

Sylvester Williams – Denver Broncos (Jefferson City)

Tim Barnes – LA Rams (Pettis County Northwest/Mizzou)

Walt Powell – Buffalo Bills (Hazelwood East)

Will Compton – Washington Redskins (North County)

FUN & GAMES

Across

1. MULTIPLE-TIME NASCAR WINNER
2. "COOL PAPA"
3. STEWART WHO WAS LONGTIME MIZZOU COACH
4. SPINKS WHO BEAT MUHAMMAD ALI FOR HEAVYWEIGHT TITLE IN 1978
5. MIZZOU FOOTBALL FIELD NAMED AFTER HIM
6. DAVIS CUP FOUNDER

Down

1. "IT AIN'T OVER TIL IT'S OVER."
2. THE "OLD PROFESSOR"
3. TOM WHO WON EIGHT PGA MAJORS
4. BRADLEY WHO PLAYED WITH THE KNICKS
5. STEWART WHO WON 1991 AND 1999 U.S. OPEN
6. "HOLY COW!" SPORTSCASTER
7. JUDY WHO PLAYED IN THE LPGA IN THE 1960S AND 70S

SHOW ME

THE DIFFERENCE

ANSWERS IN BACK OF BOOK

ANSWERS

Pages 22-25

Show Me the Difference

Pages 54-55

Outdoors Maze

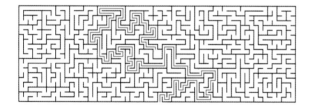

Show Me the Difference

Crossword

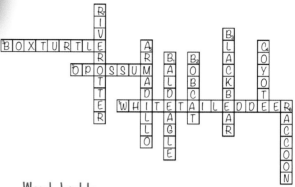

Word Jumble

1. rocanoc. . . . . raccoon
2. teoyco. . . . . coyote
3. xob utelrt . . . . box turtle
4. btcboa. . . . . bobcat
5. soopusm . . . . opossum
6. issiromu leum . . . . missouri mule
7. clkab abre. . . . . black bear
8. rwaobin tuort . . . . rainbow trout
9. sphilfddea . . . . paddlefish
10. nien-adbned imarodall . . nine-banded armadillo
11. nertaes bdeuirbl . . . . . . eastern bluebird
12. eihtw-litdae dere . . . . . . white-tailed deer
13. ierrv orett . . . . river otter

Pages 90

Pages 72-73

MO Trivia

Q: What city is known as "the Gateway to the West"? St. Louis

Q: Missouri is known as what? The Show-Me State. Some believe it began in 1899 when Congressman Willard Vandiver was quoted as saying, "I'm from Missouri and you've got to show me."

Q: What handy dessert was introduced at the 1904 St. Louis World's Fair? The ice cream cone. An ice cream vendor ran out of cups and asked a waffle vendor to roll up waffles to hold the ice cream.

Q: Samuel Clemens is known by what other name? Mark Twain

Q: What Missouri politician started out as a farmer? Harry S. Truman, thirty-third president of the United States

Q: What is the name of the Maryland-to-California route of early settlers? The National Old Trails Road. In Lexington, Missouri, the Madonna of the Trail Monument represents the women who helped conquer the West along this trail.

Q: The first successful parachute jump from an airplane was made in 1912 in which city? St. Louis

Q: Which city has more fountains than any city except Rome? Kansas City

Q: What insect was declared Missouri's state insect? The honeybee. It was declared by Governor John Ashcroft in 1985.

Q: What outlaw brothers were born in Kearney, Missouri? Jesse and Frank James

Q: What is mozarkite? The official state rock of Missouri. It was adopted by the Missouri legislature in 1967.

Q: Missouri has an official state folk dance. What is it? The square dance

Q: What is Missouri's first permanent settlement? Ste. Genevieve

Q: How many states border Missouri? Eight! Arkansas, Illinois, Iowa, Kansas, Kentucky, Nebraska, Oklahoma, Tennessee

Q: Name a drink introduced at the 1904 World's Fair. Iced tea and Dr. Pepper

Word Search

```
+ H + H + M + + + E Y + S + + R T + + +
N + C + A + A + + E N N + + + E + + + +
I + + S + R + R N + I O + + N K + + + +
P + + + U + R S K K + S L N + R + + + +
O + + + + B I Y R T U + E A + A + + + +
H + + + + D S E S S W S + + M P + + + +
C + + + T + P U A T S A + + + E + + + +
E + + L + N + N H E R M I + + I I + + +
T + A + I + B + E P A U + N + L + N + +
A W + L + L + W + Y L + M + D R + S N +
K + R + O + I + A + + O + A A A + A + A
+ A + W + L + A + + + D + N H + M + +
M + + + L + N + + + + + A I C + W + +
+ + + I H G R E B D N I L S E L R A H C
+ D A L E C A R N E G I E + L + + L + +
+ M + L D R E D S C O T T + B + + T + +
S + O N I L P O J T T O C S O + + O + +
+ U + + + + + + + + + + + + O + + N + +
+ + + + + + + + + + + + + + N + + + +
+ + + + + + + + + + + + + E + + + + +
```

Adolphus Busch (14,13,NW)
Annie Malone (20,11,NW)
Charles Lindbergh (20,14,W)
Charlie Parker (16,13,N)
Dale Carnegie (2,15,E)
Daniel Boone (15,10,S)
Dred Scott (5,16,E)
Harry S Truman (4,1,SE)
Kate Chopin (1,11,N)

Mark Twain (6,1,SE)
Marlin Perkins (1,13,NE)
Maya Angelou (12,8,SW)
Sam Walton (18,10,S)
Scott Joplin (14,17,W)
Susan Blow (12,4,SW)
Tennessee Williams (17,1,SW)
Walt Disney (2,10,NE)

Show Me the Difference

Pages 144-145

Crossword

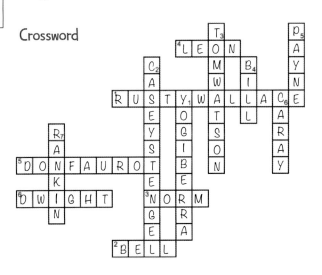

INDEX

IMAGE CREDITS

Adam Michalski: 97 (bottom right)

Adam Proctor: 79 (middle)

Amy Bautz: 6 (top right)

Animal Protective Association: 12 (bottom right)

Anirudh Koul: 132 (left), 135 (bottom)

Beth Felice: 92 (top), 94 (top)

CBS Television: 137 (top)

Charles Guggenheim: 138

Chase Candy Company: 94 (right)

Christopher Carter: 18 (bottom center)

Chuck Morris: 110 (bottom)

College Basketball Experience: 142

Daniel Schwen: 2 (top), 3 (bottom)

David Lancaster: 95, 116

David Wilson: 124 (left center)

Dickerson Park Zoo: 18 (bottom left)

Don Korte: 41 (top), 44 (left), 51 (bottom)

Endangered Wolf Center: 18 (right)

Federal Highway Administration: 126 (top)

Gateway Pet Guardians: 13 (bottom)

Georges Biard: 63 (bottom)

Grant's Farm: 19 (top left)

Green Dirt Farm: 28 (left center)

Harry Barth: 140 (left)

Humane Society of Missouri: 10 (left), 11 (top), 12 (left)

Joel Krauska: 6 (top left)

Jordon R. Beesley: 127 (inset)

Kansas City Call: 132 (right), 140 (bottom right)

Kansas City Motor Car Company: 129 (bottom right)

Kansas City Parks and Recreation: 52 (left)

Kimberly Vardeman: 97 (center inset)

Laura Lynne: 92 (right)

Library of Congress: 5 (bottom), 56 (top),

59 (top), 62, 134 (bottom right)

Los Angeles Times: 137 (bottom)

McDonnell Genome Institute: 86 (bottom left)

Megan Turner: 21

Michael Allen: 96

Michael Barera: 131 (bottom right)

Missouri History Museum Library and Archives: 60 (top), 81 (bottom)

Michael Soluri Photography: 112 (top), 119 (right)

Minneapolis Star-Journal: 130 (bottom right)

Missouri Department of Conservation: 47 (bottom right), 52 (bottom right)

Missouri Life Magazine: 102 (right)

Missouri State Archives: 107 (left), 130 (top right)

Missouri State Parks: 38 (bottom right), 43 (bottom), 44 (top), 46, 48, 49, 54

Missouri Wildlife Rescue: 8 (left), 13 (top)

Mizzou Research Site: 104 (inset)

NBC Television: 137 (left)

Nima Kasraie: 5 (top)

Paramount Pictures: 139

Paul Sableman: 78 (top), 124 (top right)

Pixabay: 8 (right), 12 (top), 16 (right), 17 (top), 20 (middle), 26, 28 (top), 32, , 34, 35, 36, 37, 38 (top), 40, 41 (left), 44 (bottom right)

PublicDomainPictures.com: 15 (bottom and top), 16 (bottom left), 17 (overlapped)

Quail Ridge Horseshoe Club: 141

Rob Kinney: 107 (right)

Robert Schediwy: 77 (bottom)

Roger Brandt: 14 (top), 19 (bottom), 21 (left center)

Saint Louis Zoo: 18 (top), 24

Shatto Milk Company: 26 (left), 29 (bottom)

Smithsonian Institution from United States: 124 (bottom right)

St. Louis County Missouri: 50

St. Louis County Parks: 19 (right)

State of Missouri: 128 (bottom)

Steve Lerro: 122 (left), 131 (top)

Tara Prosser: 10 (bottom)

TechShop: 119 (left)

Thies Farm: 28 (bottom)

Thomas Duesing: 98

Timothy Boyd: 92 (left), 97 (top)

U.S. Fish and Wildlife Service National Digital Library: 8 (top), 14 (middle), 15 (middle), 16 (top), 20 (top and bottom), 53 (top)

Vecteezy.com: Illustrations throughout book

Weston Red Barn Farm: 29 (top)

Wikimedia Commons: 11 (bottom), 45 (bottom), 61 (top), 80 (bottom left), 97 (bottom), 100, 106, 108, 109, 111 (bottom), 112 (left), 122 (top), 125, 127 (top), 128, 129, 130 (bottom), 131 (bottom left), 132 (top), 134 (bottom), 135, 136

Wikipedia: viii, 2 (bottom), 3, 4, 6 (bottom), 7, 67 (bottom), 76 (bottom left), 79 (bottom), 80, (right), 104 (left center), 114 (top)

Wildcat Glades Audubon Center: 53 (right)

William J. Clinton Presidential Library: 58 (top)

William Morris: 78 (top)

Zoo Montana: 10 (top)

Any images not listed above are believed to be in the public domain.